THE BIG THREE

TYLER STRATTON

ISBN 978-1-7326471-7-6

Printed in USA

Formatting done by Crystal Peake Type

CONTENTS

MY MESSAGE TO THE READER

Hello everyone, and welcome to my inner and outer world. My name is Tyler Joe Stratton. I am so very grateful that you have picked up this book and decided to begin this journey to discover how you can start living a better quality of life by learning how to build powerful and loving relationships with The Big Three: yourself, others and God. As I walk you through my many discoveries, I hope that my story will empower you to push yourself to the pinnacle toward your ultimate human life, teach you how to cultivate a better relationship with yourself, develop meaningful relationships with others, and help you navigate through all the roads ahead that may seem insurmountable.

Before you dive into this book, let it be known that every single one of us has the potential to live the life many will only ever dream about. Your best quality of life begins by understanding this powerful life enhance truth, which is, your overall quality of life is directly related to the quality of relationships you have with The Big Three: yourself, others, and God. And for you to make a significant change in your life and your relationships, there is something you must understand to see the results in your reality that you genuinely want to see. You must understand that the life and relationships you want to have can be created through proper repetition. For repetition is the mother of all learning, and the more you do what is in this book, the better your relationships and quality of life will become. That's why if you are looking to experience a real change in your life and gain powerful and loving relationships with yourself, others, and God, you must not think for one moment that reading this book once will suffice.

I highly recommend after digesting this book thoroughly, you put a reminder on your phone that will remind you to spend a few hours reviewing it every month. Examining this book once a month and keeping this book by your bedside or in a place where you can see it often, will help remind you that the quality of life we live directly reflects the relationships we have with The Big Three. Keeping this understanding at the forefront of your mind daily will help you continue to improve the relationships you have in your life. Please remember that the implementation and repetition of these principles can only be made permanent through constant practice and action.

I want you to be able to look back at the end of your life and see all the beautiful relationships you had and feel the love from them all. I want you to be able to look back at your life and deeply explore the love, peace, joy, and comfort that all your healthy and loving relationships have offered you. I want you to be able to look back and realize that the life you lived was a life worth reliving because of the relationships you build throughout your entire life. Because at the end of life, what matters is not what we bought, but what we created with others, not what we received, but what we've got to share, not our achievements, but our relationships we had with The Big Three.

WHY THIS BOOK

Over the years, I have discovered a lot from my internal and external suffering, which stemmed from experiencing a parental separation, being bullied, and being physically and emotionally abused. However, during the years of my suffering, the one thing that I realized, is that life doesn't have to be so miserable and hard, even when we are going through our most difficult challenges.

When it comes to relationships, too many people have just accepted that they will most likely die alone, that relationships nowadays are fake and are no longer worth the time, energy or effort we put into them. Many of these same individuals who believe this, are also the ones who have been promised a "forever" once or twice in their lives, only to find that same "forever" taken away from them out of nowhere. I too was also promised a "forever", only to find it dissolved into thin air. This ultimately left me with a lot of pain and many unanswered questions to deal with, which continually ran through my mind causing me to suffer even more.

During the times of struggle, many people seem to just run away from their problems instead of trying to face them and fix them. No one wants to face the pain it takes to heal, and many people nowadays are looking for a quick fix which often results in binge watching Netflix, constantly being on their phones and just packing up and leaving their problems behind them. I have done all three. However, what I have learned is that when the problem is you, then the problem becomes very hard to just pack up and run away from. For no matter where you go or how far you try to run, you will be stuck with yourself, whom you can't ever outrun. I have realized this the hard way.

Throughout my own journey, I've also realized that we can begin to enjoy life and live it to our fullest capability no matter what may have happened to us in the past, what is happening in the present, or what might happen in the future. Stay hopeful, my friends, because life can actually be enjoyable as long as you decide you want it to be. Before discovering how to build powerful and loving relationships with yourself, others and the Divine, there are a few things I want you to know:

The first is that, in my eyes and in my mind, I believe that we can love anyone deeply and openly. Even if we don't know them that well. I believe we can love someone just the same way we can fall in love with a puppy. I believe love is as abundant as the stars are in the sky and a feeling of positive energy that can be generated at any time we decide. So, when I talk about love, I don't only mean specifically loving your significant other; I mean loving anyone or anything as a whole. Love is abundant and forever available to all of us.

I also want you to know that when I talk about God, I am not here to point you toward any specific religion or practice. I am here to help you realize the gift of believing in God. I am here to help you build a foundational relationship with God. For I know that by building and working off of this foundation that I will lay before you, you can build a powerful and loving relationship with God, and God will help you achieve your fullest life. It is my hope by the end of this book to help you realize that God is always with you and here to support you and love you deeply. No matter what. Furthermore, it is in my greatest of all hopes that this book will help you build powerful and loving relationships with yourself, with others and with God so that you can live more confidently, courageously and joyfully! I plan to get you to this enhanced state of living by offering you the teachings and discoveries I have learned over the years from the many different experiences and mentors who have taught me how to live a better quality of life. A life where I am much happier, healthier, more positive and wealthier; mentally, spiritually, and emotionally.

The best way to live a better quality of life, is by allowing yourself to be open and vulnerable at all times so that you can continue to build powerful and loving relationships with yourself, others, and God. Without the willingness to be vulnerable, you will find it difficult to be who you were always meant to become and feel an abundance of love in your life. You will also find it hard to create powerful and loving relationships with The Big Three; yourself, others, and God. These three relationships will dictate what type of life you are going to live.

Relationships are truly everything. They make us who we are and who we are not. They make us come alive, empower us with love, connection, and wonder as well as put the greatest of all fears in our minds that stop us from being who we know we are and can be. By allowing yourself to become open to love and connect with yourself, others and God, you will be able to experience a happier, loving, and fulfilling quality of life. I promise that if you take what I am telling you to heart, that you will experience more clarity, joy, fulfillment, and love. You will also be able to open your heart and keep it open for all to enjoy.

These three relationships, if worked on and built continuously, day after day, will help you really feel what happiness, connection, love, joy and fulfillment are all about when lived fully. You will then be able to step into a life with more confidence, courage, and a loving heart.

Finally, this book will help you transition from a state of loneliness, sadness and depression, to a state of connection, joy and fulfillment. It will help you realize that relationships are everything, and that your entire life is, and will always be, wrapped around these three relationships. And if you can learn to build these three relationships (which is what I will teach you how to do), then you will begin to experience a life full of joy, fulfillment, love, connection and aliveness. I cannot express this enough!

By empowering yourself with the knowledge of how to be someone who is successful at building and sustaining long-term relationships, you will then begin to experience the best life and overcome many of life's greatest struggles. When you are equipped with a strong self-worth, supportive relationships and a loving God, anything becomes possible.

May you be blessed, healed, fully loved, and ready to change your life for the better. With all the love in the world, may your journey toward a better quality of life be filled with hope, love, and light!

BACKSTORY: MY CHILDHOOD & FIRST HEARTBREAK

Regardless of who you are or your personal beliefs, the key to long-term success in life is creating powerful and loving relationships with yourself, others, and the Divine. Unfortunately, I didn't know this when my heart broke into a thousand pieces as the people I loved the most, seemed to break it the most. Throughout my entire life, relationships have been a consistent, heart-breaking struggle that has resulted in many years of misery, counseling and a lower quality of life.

At the young age of four, I experienced my first heartbreak. Of course, at that time I didn't know what a heartbreak was. What I did know, however, was that the feeling I had on that cold September night as my parents' marriage was coming to an ugly end, was the absolute worst feeling I had ever felt in my four short years on Earth.

As the heartbreaking night went on, all I wanted was for this emotional pain I was experiencing to end, but no matter what I tried to do, nothing could make this feeling simmer down and this night end quick enough. The internal pain that I was feeling was unlike any other feeling I have ever experienced. It was like a cancer that consumed my entire being, which took the life and energy right out of me. Feeling very lost, broken, weak, angry, and scared as my parents fight continued on, I remember not wanting to move or make a sound. All I knew was that I never wanted to experience those feelings ever again. As the fighting continued through the night, I found myself becoming more and more overwhelmed by all the yelling. I was too afraid to make any noise and very confused about why the people I loved the most seemed to be hurting me the most.

As the night went on as if it was never going to end, my fears of separation began to deepen. That night was the night that would become the turning point of my life and change how I would go out into this world and treat myself, others, and God.

Between the time of my parent's separation and high school, life wasn't the best. It was the years after my parent's divorce that caused me to suffer the most. Those were the years when I dealt with a lot of loneliness, feelings of separation, anger and depression, which led to vivid thoughts of suicide. All of these feelings started to consume me entirely and began to bring on a negative mindset that caused me to ponder if ending it all was the only way out of all the internal pain and suffering.

As these terrible thoughts and images ran through my mind, I began to distance myself away from the deep and loving relationships with those who mattered the most. As these negative thoughts started to become my reality, I began to lose myself and rebel. I neglected my health, began to act badly toward others and separate myself from God.

It's crazy what a separation of any kind can do to your mind, your body and your spirit. This separation, and everything in between it and high school, really molded me into becoming a person who I could no longer recognize, and I found myself with a negative outlook on life. This negative outlook on life began to consume every part of my entire being.

To this day, I still remember sitting in front of my aunt's television visualizing myself with a gun in my mouth pulling the trigger. Even though I knew these were terrible thoughts, I still never told anyone. I was too afraid to admit that at the young age of eight; I was suffering this badly. And no one knew how badly I was hurting, for I never allowed the deep pain to show itself when I was around others. I believe the reason that I kept it to myself, was because I never felt like anyone would understand what I was going through or care enough to listen. I mean, my parents didn't care how I felt when they decided to separate, so why would they or anyone else care now?

As the days, weeks, months and many years continued, I still found myself after school, sitting in front of the same television at my aunt's house, visualizing my own death and imagining what life would be like without all of this pain and suffering I was experiencing.

Eventually, these scary thoughts began to cripple me mentally, and I felt hopeless in escaping this state of mind. It was like waking up from a nightmare and hearing something move in your room. It paralyzed me. I was so afraid that I tried to act as if it didn't happen. But I couldn't escape these thoughts and feelings any longer, and so they consumed every bit of who I was.

As I continued to hold on to these painful feelings because of the past, my hate towards God and others continued to grow, and it greatly affected my quality of life throughout my childhood. I never allowed myself to let go of the past, live in the now, and build a brighter tomorrow. This alone is a huge reason why I couldn't live a better quality of life and a reason why many of you might not be able to either. My inability to forgive and let go of all the hurt and pain created a man who was not open to accepting and experiencing a better quality of life or love. This lack of a joy and love was the reason I wouldn't allow myself to create loving relationships with myself, with others and with God. I was too afraid to allow anyone back into my heart and love became my enemy.

It is astounding what one broken relationship can do to you, especially as a child. Because of this painful divorce, growing up was a tough experience for me. I felt a deep and profound loneliness which would later discourage me from sharing my life with anyone, and as time went on, my suffering continued, and my rebellion got worse. My feelings negatively affected my life so much that my family decided to put me in counseling. This was not what I wanted; to talk to someone about why I was an eight-year-old kid who would not allow intimate relationships to be formed in his life.

Discussing my personal issues with someone else was not my cup of tea. But I was no longer able to hide my pain, and I soon discovered that the more I ran away from The Big Three–myself, others and God, the more lifeless I felt. Pushing out all meaningful relationships, I became deeply depressed and more miserable. **After many years of counseling, I began to uncover my inner truth.**

Counseling helped me to discover and understand what I was experiencing internally and how to overcome some of the pain. Perhaps professional help was what I needed. After many years of counseling, I can honestly say that it did, in fact, help me considerably. However, what I didn't acquire, was the ability to cope with my pain for a long period of time. Eventually, I sought out my own means of coping.

During my quest toward finding long-term peace, I did discover something that I was sure would ease this pain and help me feel more peaceful. I discovered the game of football. Football, to me, became the means of coping that I had been searching for, and the game that I would end up playing for the next eight years of my life.

It appeared to be exactly what I needed to "heal" my hurt and build the relationships I never had. I believe that the reasons why I loved football so much, and why I stuck with it for so long, were because of how connected I felt while playing, and how powerful the relationships with my coaches and teammates had become. It was the feeling of winning and constantly improving my athletic ability that helped me to feel good about who I was becoming.

It was the coaches who helped me to understand that having faith in God can move all doubt filled days, and it was my teammates who helped me get through the dark times in my life. Football became the best coping mechanism I would ever use. More importantly, football was there for me when I was at my worst, and that is why I never gave up on it.

The game of football allowed me to express who I was and how I was feeling. It accepted my pain and encouraged me to express it. It allowed me to take all the years of my suffering that I had been holding onto for so long out onto the field and just let it all go. It allowed me to release my pain and suffering without revealing it or hurting anyone. It temporarily removed all the years of feeling separated, lost, depressed, and alone.

THE POWER OF INTERNAL PAIN

My internal pain drove me to become the joyful man I am today and the elite athlete I was in high school. The psychological and emotional pain that I dealt with for many years was far worse than any amount of physical pain that I would ever feel in any sport I played. That is why I let the internal pain drive me to become the elite athlete I was.

It was this internal pain that allowed me to run the ball with a fearless heart, never being afraid to feel any type of physical pain. You see, in high school, I was the type of running back that never used many moves when it came to avoiding the defenders who stood in my way. I was the type of running back that would run through a man before I would try going around him.

The type who would lower his shoulder and meet the hit head on, rather than try to put on fancy moves. I would run the ball with the mindset that no amount of physical pain could ever surpass the amount of mental suffering I had endured. I ran the ball fearlessly. The great thing about the game of football was it gave me the chance I needed to relieve my pain, and to leave my reality behind for a little while. It was the escape that I needed to find a little bit of peace.

Being a running back really helped me to relieve my past pains that had chained me down for so long, and it was a gift only God knew I needed at that time. As football became a more integral part of who I was, and a defining characteristic of my life, I became much happier, healthier and positive. I finally felt like I was living life more fully, I had a purpose, and had others who cared about me. I finally felt like I was a part of a great group of guys who made me feel like I was family. A real family. A family who would stick together even when times would get hard. A family where trust was built and kept. A family where laughter and stories were shared, and memories were created. Football was my family.

Allowing football into my life eventually allowed me to become more open to developing a better quality of life and I began to build meaningful relationships with others outside of my team. It helped me to understand what trust was, build my faith, feel heard by others, and more importantly, to understand commitment. With football, I discovered just how powerful and helpful long-term and deep relationships can really be. Which is exactly what I needed to learn and embrace before entering high school.

HIGH SCHOOL AND THE SECOND HEARTBREAK

High school came around, and boy, was that a great feeling. I had been anticipating those years for such a long time. These were the years that mattered the most, especially as an athlete. As I entered high school, I really felt like my life was beginning to take a step in the right direction. Keeping my focus on the game, rather than on my past, I did everything I could to become a recognizable asset to the team and to my school.

During those few years of being a part of a great team, my mind and my emotions finally began to heal. As my heart and mind became healthier, I desired something greater than what any sport had ever been able to offer me. Football had given me the courage I needed in order to become open to the most divine of all feelings; love. And this was what I desired more than anything as I stepped into high school.

During my eleventh grade year, I discovered that love meant everything to me. That it was love that I was truly after in life. Not fame, fortune, or to even be a recognizable asset to the team. And with this newfound understanding and healing that took place, what I began to really understand was what my heart was yearning for. I became aware that my soul was searching for a powerful relationship with a foundation that was built on love.

I wanted a deeper understanding of how to love myself and others. I wanted to love deeply and to be loved, the same way a mother loves her child, a dog loves their owner, and the way that God loves his people. This was the type of love and relationship my soul was after.

As I began to open myself back up to love, I felt how powerful it was to fall in love with someone and have them fall in love with me. This feeling was an inexplicable feeling. Falling in love was a truly incredible and wonderful blessing. Until once again, it wasn't so wonderful. As I said before, relationships throughout my entire life have been a consistent, heartbreaking struggle, causing me many years of misery.

One afternoon, while hanging out and talking to a few of my football buddies, I was informed that the girl who I was with throughout high school had crossed all lines of loyalty and cheated on me. The pain from hearing that news struck my heart hard and fast and instantly caused so many negative emotions to explode from within me.

These past emotions started their journey from my heart and quickly escalated into my mind and began weakening my body and destroying my soul. My childhood feelings of depression, anger, sadness and separation quickly reentered my world as though they had never left. Once again, in a blink of an eye, I was cast into the lonely dark wilderness and misery of my childhood.

Too weak-minded and too afraid to be by myself and alone with my thoughts again, we ended up getting back together and found ourselves on and off for three years. This heartbreak wasn't easy to overcome. It was one of the most challenging things I had to figure out how to overcome.

However, I am truly grateful for all the hardship and struggles that I had to face during those three years. For if it wasn't for everything that I went through, I wouldn't be where I am today. It was during those tough times that my suffering became my teacher. I became the student learning about my suffering, so that I could one day, not only live a better quality of life but also help others learn how to experience the beauty of life by teaching them how to build powerful and loving relationships with themselves, others and God.

As I look back, I will never regret what I went through as a child or what I went through during my heartbreak, for I am exactly where God always intended me to be. And every troubling time was a true blessing in disguise. For the lessons I have discovered along the way, have helped pull me toward the biggest shift that has ever taken part in my life.

THE BIG SHIFT THAT STARTED WITH A DECISION

> "Relationships, not achievements or the acquisition of things, are what matters most in life."
>
> — RICK WARREN.

A big shift began to take place in my mind, heart and soul. After the official break up, I made the committed and firm decision to finally take control of my life and not allow myself to experience this type of low quality of life any longer. It was challenging to get to this point, but it was a point in which everyone will eventually come to. I made this committed and firm decision once I realized it was me who was causing myself to suffer.

The more I learned about my suffering and what caused it, the more I realized that it was I who caused all my suffering. This was a big bite that was very hard to chew. But

I knew I was tired of suffering and sick knowing that I was the one who caused myself to suffer way too long!

This internal suffering was consuming me to the point I found myself contemplating life. I concluded, that after many years of living in my inner world with misery, suffering, depression and loneliness, that it was time to stop telling myself and others that I was doing just fine. Saying you are fine when you are not is the easiest way to stay in your suffering. Let yourself heal by being clear with yourself and with others that you are not okay.

Making the committed decision to fully accept my suffering and allow others into my life set me up on the right path toward deep internal healing. This commitment helped me to accept my pain, grow through it, and learn a better way to cope with my issues, rather than try to hide them from others and avoid them by taking them out on a football field.

I was so fed up with running away from the pain, not being happy, living a low quality of life and trying to avoid the misery by putting on a fake smile and pretending that I was someone who I was not. I was tired of giving my life away to misery, and I was sick of feeling drained all the time because of how much energy and effort I had to give to others to hide who I really was and how I was really feeling.

It was during this time that I discovered that my spiritual tank was on empty and that I had finally used up all of my energy in an effort to convince others that I was okay. Without the energy that I needed to keep me from running away from the truth and the pain that I was dealing with, I decided to do something I had never done before; accept the truth and start fixing it.

Once I opened myself back up to the loving relationships that were still in my life, I became courageous and confident enough to challenge myself and begin to change. I learned to accept who I was and began learning how to fix the inner and outer issues I had been experiencing throughout most of my life.

However, I could have never done this alone. It was through the help of my mother, father, friends and, most importantly, my brother who helped me to heal. It was their unconditional love and advice that helped me find my inner peace and joy.

But it wasn't until my brother introduced me to something so powerful that my life truly began to drastically change and transform. It was my brother's advice that catapulted me into the direction that had actually led me to not only heal myself but also help others and write this book. It was my brother who advised me to read a life-changing book with him.

Now up to this point, I hated reading! I was illiterate and had a very bad taste in my mouth from all the years of tutoring I had to go through. But at this point in my life, I would do anything that I could to stop the suffering. Including reading. When he handed me the giant book, the first thought I had was there is no way in heck I will be able to finish this book! However, in just two weeks, I had finished this life-changing book and found myself in a new state of mind!

And I discovered the power of reading, and specifically, the power of self-help books and how much of an impact they can have on your life. The book my brother had me read with him, and my first self-help book that I finished, was titled, The Law of Success. From the 1925, Manuscript Lessons, by Napoleon Hill.

This was the book that changed my life drastically! I dove into this powerful book and found myself craving to discover many other great "How to" books on success, relationships, living in the moment, love, and personal freedom. I drowned myself in personal development books and learned so much on these topics and issues. And once I began to implement these teachings in my life, I started to feel better about who I was and began to see life differently and heal faster.

After finishing my first self-help book, I decided to

commit myself to building a better future, a better life and more importantly a stronger me. It became my passion to build a life full of real success, where joy, gratitude, fulfillment, confidence, purpose, and love would be a part of who I was and who people would see me as.

After reading many books, listening to many podcasts, and going to different seminars, I realized that I could build the life of powerful and loving relationships with myself, others and God, that I had always wanted. I discovered the truth about life, and how anyone could eventually become their best version of themselves and live the life they had always believed they deserved to live.

Now while pursuing these avenues of self-help, I decided that the information which I was acquiring was just too valuable to keep to myself, and that's when I made it my mission to not only help myself, but others as well. **I knew where my happiness was, and I knew that true happiness entered my heart when I offered a helping hand to others**. I knew that true love would fill my heart when I offered my best and true self to others.

Discovering these two truths encouraged me to continue learning everything I could about relationships, love, joy and happiness, and how to live the best life possible. What I found, after many years of studying, was that one's fullest potential can be unlocked and reached if they understand the power of relationships and understand that relationships directly reflect your overall quality of life you live.

Learning how to build powerful and loving relationships with yourself, others and the Divine, will help you achieve your fullest life possible. A life full of powerful and loving relationships is a life where everyday happiness, joy, gratitude, connection, success, wealth, and love are possible. Do yourself a powerful favor and surround yourself and build those relationships that reflect who you want to be and how you want to feel. Don't allow those who you associate with to influence your life in a negative manner.

Life is as beautiful as the relationship you allow and have in your life. Relationships are the greatest empires that you should be continually building and growing. For if you can do that, you can live a life full of real success and joy.

The relationship you have with yourself, others and God, will one day become more important to you than any amount of money or material possessions, so you may as well do yourself a favor and learn how to build your fullest life and achieve true success right now. For the life that is waiting for you on the other side of powerful and loving relationships, is one of pure beauty, love and aliveness.

What many people consider important right now, won't matter in the end, and what actually does matter are the types of relationships you have learned to grow and sustain. If you are ready to live a more meaningful and better quality of life and learn how you can reach your full potential, then stick around. What I have for you in this book will be life-changing. There is a beautiful life out there waiting for you to create and experience. If I can do it and live it, I know you can learn it and live it too.

PART I

KEY #1: BUILDING YOURSELF

"The most powerful relationship you will ever have is the relationship you have with yourself, for it will set the tone for every other relationship you will ever have."

— TYLER JOE STRATTON

Your relationship with yourself is arguably the most important relationship in life. The relationship you have with yourself is the foundation of everything else. Before you can create a better quality of life and the healthy relationship that you want with others, you first need to work *on you*. When you work on yourself, the goal is to get to know who you really are and then live genuinely, authentically and congruently as yourself. And to live genuinely, authentically and congruently as yourself, is to be in control of your fears, thoughts and emotions. But in order to be in control of your fears, thoughts and emotions, one needs to learn to create a strong and clear vision.

When you create a strong and clear vision that raises the standards to which you hold yourself, you will not only raise the standards of the relationship you have with yourself, but you will also help bring out the best in life, in your partner and create a deeper relationship with God.

Over the years, I have dug deep in order to really understand the relationship I had with myself, and how it was reflecting on my relationships with my overall quality of life, others and God. However, in understanding myself, I discovered that I only really understood who I was after I destroyed myself. And only during the process of repairing myself, did I learn who I was truly meant to be.

Now, I don't recommend you do the same. I am just informing you that it was after I hit rock bottom that I started to learn who I was and was not, what I was about and who I wanted to become. While sitting at rock bottom, examining my relationship with myself, I realized that it was the only constant relationship I would ever have in my entire life. I also discovered that this relationship would also be a direct reflection of the relationships I had with everyone and everything else.

This discovery was very terrifying, for I realized that this relationship was the worst of the three, and that the relationship I have with myself would determine my overall quality of relationships I had throughout my life.

At the time of this discovery, my relationship with myself was one of pure self-torture. I had no confidence; I was heartbroken, very negative, and hopeless. I found that I became angry with myself and depressed about the life that I was given. I was the victim who only saw how cruel this world and the people in it was. I never found life to be fair, joyful, or loving. How miserable that was.

The relationship you have with yourself determines many outcomes, because life itself is only ever experienced

through your own self and your own eyes. Meaning, your perception of who you believe you are, will ultimately determine how you will experience life. Therefore, if you want to live life to its fullest, then you must learn how to develop a powerful and loving relationship with yourself. You must learn to take care of yourself in a meaningful and purposeful way. You must learn to live in congruence to who you know you can be and show up as that. Ultimately, learning to love and accept who you are, is the best thing you can ever do for yourself.

1

IT'S YOUR CHOICE

> "When you start taking care of yourself you start feeling better, you start looking better, and you start to attract a better quality of life. It all starts within you."
>
> — TYLER JOE STRATTON

The relationship with yourself might just be one of the most important and meaningful relationships you will ever have in your entire life. For it is this relationship that will set the tone for the type of life you are going to live. It's this relationship that will either empower you or destroy you. It's all in the way you see yourself, treat yourself and talk to yourself that will determine the type of life you are going to live.

The best part about this relationship is that you get to choose what type of relationship this will be. You have the power and free will to choose to either have a loving relationship or a hateful relationship with yourself. The choice you make will ultimately reflect the type of life you will see.

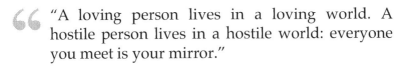 "A loving person lives in a loving world. A hostile person lives in a hostile world: everyone you meet is your mirror."

— KEN KEYES JR.

I believe we can all experience a sense of our own heaven and our own hell as we walk with ourselves through our daily life. We can either walk in the valley of darkness or walk in the clouds of light. Just remember, as you wake up each and every day, you have a very important choice to make.

You get to choose whether you will be happy today or miserable today. You get to choose to either live a life that will bring you joy, fulfillment, purpose and love, or you can choose one full of misery. Everyone you meet is just a reflection of yourself. Make the choice to be the light you need in your own life and watch those around you become the light that you are.

Like many others, I have walked both paths. However, for most of my life, the relationship I had with myself was walked in the valley of darkness. For many years I consistently felt sad, separated, and quite lonely. Some moments it affected me in a subtle way and others in a great way. But because many of us are affected by sadness, separation and loneliness in times of turmoil or loss, I want to discuss the times when I felt the same pain during subtle events that took place.

For example, throughout my childhood and teen years, I suffered from separation. I remember the nights I would play Xbox live with my childhood friends for hours on end to just avoid the feeling of separation and being alone. There were times I would spend eight to twelve hours a day on the weekends playing video games with them. This video game addiction was only there to help me avoid the pain that I was really feeling and dealing with.

I would do everything in my power to keep my friends from going offline. I found myself missing doctor appointments, not doing my homework, and sometimes not even eating, just so I didn't have to let them go or go offline and experience the feeling of them "leaving me". The feelings I would feel every time my friends went offline would instantly make me feel sad, separated and lonely. These feelings showed up for many more years, no matter how great or subtle the separation was. It could have been a break up or a friend leaving my house after they had spent the night. No matter how great or how little the separation was, I would always find myself feeling sad and lonely.

However, as years went by and I continued to learn and grow as a young adult, I discovered the reason why I felt this way and learned how to not feel so sad and lonely when separations took place. What I learned throughout my years of continuous self-discovery, was the reason why I felt the way I did was because of the choices I made.

You see, it was where I decided to focus my attention that made me feel the way I felt. I put my attention on the separation of them always leaving and not on the abundance of fun and connection we had while we were together. I realized that it was the choice of deciding where I would focus my attention that would cause me to live in a negative world. It was this choice I made that caused a lot of pain.

I learned that I was the co-creator of my reality and I held the power to either choose to see the positive or the negative in every situation. The moment I realized this truth, I began to forcefully fight back for my inner peace and joy that I wanted to feel every time my mind would automatically find the negative.

Now, after learning more about myself as time goes on, I

have found that both paths are so beautiful to walk. For it is in my darkest times that I have learned to understand myself, and in my brightest days that I have been able to enjoy myself. However, no matter what path you are walking, I want you to know that you must learn to make a clear choice. To either walk with a clear vision and a purpose or walk in an autonomous mode allowing life to happen to you.

For if you can do what I did and begin to wake up every day, create a vision for yourself and set the intention to create a purposeful relationship with yourself, you will start to live a life that is more fulfilling! It's really that simple. You just have to decide! You must take a stand as a giant and walk like a lion through every path you travel. No matter where you are in your life, or what you are going through, here is what I promise you: If you can refocus your attention on the positive, create a clear vision for who you want to be, and live out that vision, the relationship you have with yourself will propel you into being the best you that you can be and help you get through those terrible and tough times.

Without setting your intentions and having a vision or an understanding of what type of relationship you want to have with yourself, you will feel bullied by life and people every day. I am here to help prevent the feeling that life is in control of you and beating you up, causing you to lose hope, feel separated and feel like you are not enough.

By constantly nurturing this powerful and loving relationship with yourself, you will also be able to build the courage and confidence you need in order to go after your dreams as well as create powerful and loving relationships with others and God. Many people do not realize just how powerful and important having a relationship with yourself truly is. Nor do they truly understand what life can become like once you do have a healthy relationship with yourself. And I didn't either until I had nothing left in me and there were only two options; keep living in misery and allow life to bully me or give it one last shot and create a better life.

I am here today to let you know that by strengthening your relationship with yourself, you can make a lasting and powerful change in your life. By choosing to build this relationship, you will be able to live a life that is worth living and one that will bring you so much love, peace, joy, fulfillment and purpose.

While you are out there going through whatever you are going through, know that you are not alone, and I AM HERE for you. I am here for your heart, your mind, your soul and your life. I care about you, and that is why I've spent many hours diving deep into my studies; so that I could write this book and show you that your life can be improved and is worth improving.

There are so many benefits you will receive once you begin to build that powerful and loving relationship with yourself. I believe we can all agree that creating and strengthening loving and powerful relationships with others can be a pain. Especially when our relationship with ourselves isn't where we know it could and should be. It can be extremely difficult to create healthy relationships with others and the Divine when we are not entirely happy with who we are as an individual.

There are so many different ways in which you can work on developing a powerful and loving relationship with yourself. What I am about to share with you in the following pages, is what I found to be the most important part of building a life that will bring you all the wonderful feelings that we are supposed to experience.

2

BEFORE YOU HELP OTHERS HELP YOURSELF

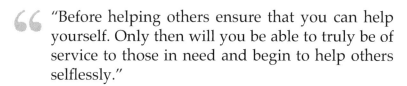

"Before helping others ensure that you can help yourself. Only then will you be able to truly be of service to those in need and begin to help others selflessly."

— TYLER JOE STRATTON

As babies, we have these natural tendencies to always put ourselves before others. We feel that our lives are worth putting before others, and that if our needs are not met, it will only cause us to suffer. That is why, as children, we often put ourselves first. However, as we got older and learned from others, one of the things we learned was that putting ourselves first was selfish and self-destructive. In other words, putting ourselves before others isn't something we should do.

As time went on, most of us adapted to this new idea that said we shouldn't put others before ourselves. But by doing so many of us became selfless, which then caused many to feel lost and frustrated, especially when trying to care for other's needs before our own. I am not saying that caring for others is not important. For I believe that being a caring person is what we should all strive to become more of. Because the truth is, this world needs more people who share this beautiful characteristic with one another.

But in order for us to be more loving and caring toward one another, we must put ourselves before others. Let me explain. We must realize that taking care of ourselves is also very important, just as we did as children. Think about the damage that we cause to ourselves and others when we don't take care of ourselves first.

For example: how many times have you been in the middle of doing something important and you get interrupted by someone asking you to do something for them? And then your internal frustration at this interruption caused you to become upset with them just because they asked for your help with a situation?

I know when I don't take care of myself first, I can become irritable, frustrated and overwhelmed. Unable to take care of your own needs and wants first, will do this to you. It will eventually cause you to lash out at someone and later regret it. It will cause you to never feel completely fulfilled or focused.

Always putting others and deadlines before yourself will cause you to feel as though you never truly lived your life. You see, I was the type of person who would always put others needs and wants before my own, no matter what I had going on. For I believed it was always the right thing to do. If another is in need, you be there for them. Pretty simple concept to live by, right? I thought this concept was simple to live by until life began to become busier and busier.

Throughout my college years, I would find myself stretched out way to thin most days. There were many weeks and months on end where I would find myself completely exhausted from working a full-time job. I'd then go home to do the normal things like cook, shower, clean, and pack my things up for the next workday, to then find myself behind my computer for many hours on end to complete my weekly college work and projects that were due.

Of course, that wasn't all I did. On top of a full-time job and college, I was also writing this book, running a side business with my brother, in a happy and healthy relationship with my girlfriend, working out five days a week, running a weekly podcast and constantly helping those who were in need. This was a lot for me to handle.

As time went on and I kept moving everything forward, one thing began to finally slip and slowly diminish, my relationship with myself. I began to slowly lose my sanity and more importantly my health. I felt overwhelmed, stressed, anxious, worried and unhealthy. This is not a place you want to find yourself. Every time I found myself in this state of negativity, my relationships with myself, others and the Divine would suffer.

I would be short with those I loved, I wouldn't want to help others no matter the task, and I was just living an unhappy life. All because I never put myself before others and all the busyness that was going on in my life. The busier I got, the less me time I had and the less me time I had, the less happy I felt.

Stepping out of high school, my brother and I started a small merchant processing and website design and development company. During the wild process of building our company together, I noticed that as money started to come in and we became busier; I had less time for myself and because of this, my relationship with myself, my brother and others got worse. The more tasks piled up, the more irritable and grumpier I became around him, especially when he would ask me to do something for the business.

When he would ask me to take care of a business task, I would become so frustrated with him just because I didn't want to help him with the business, and because it wasn't on my time and when I wanted to do it. What I really wanted to do was just take care of me and put me first. But this was hard to do as we got busier and busier within the business. The money was good, but my relationship with myself and those I cared about was not. I really thought that my brother and the business was the problem. That is until I started to look deep within myself again.

As I began to do another dive into myself, trying to figure out the problem, I realized that I was the problem behind the smaller issue. I realized that it wasn't my brother who was causing me the problem or any other external factor; it was I who was causing myself the issue.

Let us not be our own problem. Let us begin to take care better care of ourselves so that we won't be a problem to others. Let us be the solution to our problems, so we can help others with their problems. The best way that we can help others is by learning to help ourselves first.

Once you build a powerful and loving relationship with yourself, and become who you always knew you were, by waking up each morning and defining who you are and how you will consciously act that day then you will really be able to care for others more deeply, and become very successful and wholehearted in caring for them and yourself. It's such a beautiful way to live. It took me a very long time to realize that the biggest part of my past pain and suffering came from the lack of a powerful and loving relationship with myself. I am here to help you take back your life by showing you the steps you must take in order to live your life to the fullest.

3

THE PERSON YOU WERE MEANT TO BE

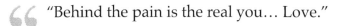 "Behind the pain is the real you… Love."

— Tyler Joe Stratton

Oh, how happy is the one who has a clear vision? A clear vision that will lead them to their final destination. But how lost is the one who is running with no clear vision, direction or goal? When it comes to understanding how to build a powerful and loving relationship with yourself, you must understand how to create a clear vision.

The clearer the vision you create for yourself, the better chance you have in order to become who you were always meant to be. No matter what you are building, whether it be a successful relationship or a successful business, you must start off by spending some time alone to create a clear vision for yourself.

If you have no vision, you will find yourself just wondering through life feeling a bit off course and lost, time and time again throughout your building process. Not knowing who you want to be or where you want to end up, could put you in a place you might not want to be. You may even find yourself being someone you know deep down you are not.

Living a life that is incongruent to who you know you can be, will be a life you will one day regret. Learn to live more congruently everyday by deciding what it is and who it is you desire to be and just be it. In other words, if you want to be happy, just be happy. Decide to be happy. It is that simple.

Once you make that decision, you must be who you think you would be if you were much happier. You must uncover and paint a clear picture of what it looks like, feels like and is like to be happy then start being that.

The first step you must learn to take when it comes to creating this powerful and loving relationship with yourself, is to get to know yourself on a deeper level, by creating a clear vision, and answering a few questions that will lead you down the path of clarity.

I want you to spend some time today to dive deeper into the depths of your soul. I want you to spend some time and go further than you have ever gone before. I want you to sit in silence for as long as you need to in order to discover who you are and who you want to become. I want you to go deeper than just your basic identity, such as your name, sex, and age. I want you to become familiar with who you truly are, not the person who people think you are or who you portray yourself as to others.

We all have one mission while we are here on Earth and that mission is to remember who we are and what we are here to do. I have learned throughout my many years of search and destroy, that you will begin to discover who you truly are when you allow yourself to go behind all the trenches of your pain and the masks that you wear.

Your true authentic self lies behind all the pain that you have been hiding from yourself and keeping from others.

When you begin to understand this truth, you must do what many people try to avoid doing. Instead of running away from your pain or hiding it through a way of coping with it, I want you to encourage yourself to walk into your pain. That's right, I want you to notice what has been causing you your pain, and what has been stopping you from being your authentic self.

It's time you courageously notice your pain and allow it to surface once again. I know it can be hard to allow your past pains to reveal their ugly selves again, but the only way to find yourself is to allow them to surface and work through them. The only way to experience and be who you were always meant to be is by becoming aware of your pain.

This will help you to discover who you are and then allow you to create a stronger vision for yourself. Please understand that what you may find during your deep dive may be shocking to you. But keep your heart and mind open to what you will find, and trust in your heart, that what you find is who you really are. For what I found after my search was scary but beautiful.

While on your exploration to remembering who you are, be aware of what you are feeling. It may be scary, but that's okay. Getting to know anyone on a deeper level is scary. So, while discovering who you are, pay close attention to your own feelings and don't be afraid, because you are only learning and uncovering more about who you truly are.

Feel your feelings. Cry your cries. Laugh your laughs. Honor your truth. Then when all the emotions are done, be still and sit in silence. Enjoy the quality time with yourself. One thing I've learned that has worked for me, is spending quality time with myself.

Quality time with yourself means no phone, no people, no distractions. This means that you should find time to drop whatever it is you might be doing and just spend a few minutes with yourself on a daily basis. Put on some music, lie down, and let your thoughts and emotions dive into the depths of your being.

This concept is best known as self-observation. I have found that the best way to discover myself and to practice self-observation, has been to go into the wilderness or a park, and just enjoy nature and reconnect with the environment. Once I step into nature and tune into the perfection of nature, I feel very supported, loved, connected and at peace with who and what I am.

However, in this busy world that we live in, it can be hard to treat yourself that nicely. So, I have learned that by giving myself only a few moments, I can still enjoy the same benefits as when visiting nature. During these moments of self-observation and discovery, I begin to observe and assess many different things in my life, such as my behaviors, my thoughts, my emotions, my beliefs and begin to ask the bigger questions in life that many avoid asking.

Asking these bigger than life questions have helped me to learn a lot about myself. Spending a few minutes each day to ask myself who am I and who do I want to be has really helped me to discover the endless possibilities of who I can become and how much I can grow as a person.

Giving yourself these few minutes each day, to step away from everyone and everything, will add up quickly and help lead you into a better understanding of who you are, and allow you to give yourself the self-care your heart, mind and body may need.

Inside every single one of us, behind the closed doors that we no longer like to open or allow others to see into, is a part of us that realizes what is best for us and what we need to let go of and begin to do to be who we truly are.

However, what most of us do in this crazy world that never sleeps, is get all caught up in the daily grind of our busy lives. We stay distracted so we don't have to face these tough questions and find those uncomfortable answers. We stay so busy, so we don't have to face the truth that we simply don't like who we are or where we are going.

We keep ourselves so busy, so we don't have to see that we have no idea who we are, what we are here to do or what our purpose is in life. Because of this, we never set time for ourselves to relax, let go, and ponder painful thoughts and emotions. Then suddenly, life passes us by in the blink of an eye, and all those painful events and moments that you haven't found time to let go of, build up quickly and will leave you unable to enjoy life fully and freely.

How can we finally enjoy our lives to the fullest? What is the best way to take care of ourselves? How can we dig ourselves out of the hole we've found ourselves in? How can we slow down the suffering and increase the joy and love much quicker? How can I become the person who I was meant to become?

I promise you this, if you can stop distracting yourself from facing yourself, you can find your true authentic and loving self, hidden behind the pain and distraction. Some of you may find it hard to face yourself and your pain alone long enough to find yourself. I know I sure had a very tough time taking my own advice. I knew I needed to spend time alone, but I also knew I didn't feel strong enough to do that so I could find myself. So, what did I do in the times of trying to discover myself and face myself?

I not only ran but sprinted into the arms of another girl to take care of me during my toughest times. For I thought that there was nothing more powerful than a woman's caring heart, and that's what I became addicted to as I noticed my own pain.

Being an addict isn't fun. I don't care what you are addicted to; it isn't easy to break the addiction. But I knew that I had to break the addiction, because if I didn't, I would never heal my pains and find who I was meant to be. I would never live my fullest life and stop breaking the hearts of others.

That is why I emphasize the importance of self-observation. Take time during each day to discover something new and interesting about yourself. Ask yourself those tough questions. Take time to discover all of the good and all of the bad. Enjoy the moments you allow a negative thought to surface. Allowing them to surface allows you to let go of them. And when you allow yourself to let go of them, who you are will become much clearer.

One way to let go of those negative emotions and thoughts when they arise, is to take a moment to write down what you have discovered about yourself during those few moments of self-observation. Take a moment each day to journal about the pains and blessings that have surfaced. At the end of each week, reflect upon the changes you need to make to enhance your sense of well-being. Write down these changes, and then commit to addressing them by encouraging yourself to take better care of yourself, and your own needs and wants.

Doing this on a daily and weekly basis will make a huge difference in your life. It might take time, but I promise you will discover who you truly are. For the more you learn about yourself, the better the relationship you will have with yourself, others and God. The better the relationship you have with yourself, others and God, the more you will be able to accept who you are and who you were always meant to become.

Accepting yourself is such a wonderful blessing to receive. I have learned this to be true, because most people will treat others how they treat themselves. As a man who has a dream bigger than himself, I am very critical with my own behaviors. And while being so critical of my own behaviors, I am also very critical of the behaviors of my closest friends and family, which isn't healthy and is something I will forever be working on. This criticism of myself has negatively affected all of my relationships. I have lost a few really good friends and the connection I once had with God.

I have accused God of giving me a bad day or life. However, as I began to practice these same steps that I am teaching you, I realized that I was becoming more tolerable toward myself and learning more about who I am. I also realized that I was becoming more tolerant of others, and that others were reciprocating this respect to me.

Respect and accept who you are, and others will do the same! The following pages will show you how to prevent the pain, suffering and negative emotions, and become who you were meant to be. Here is what you can do.

4

BUILDING A HOUSE INTO A HOME FROM THE INSIDE OUT

 "The strongest home is built from the inside out."

— TYLER JOE STRATTON

With a clear vision established in your life, your dreams about who you are and what you want to become can be achieved. The relationship you have with yourself can be anything you want it to be. It can be a relationship that is full of love and joy as long as you're willing to commit to one thing. You must make it your everyday duty to be the main source of your joy and love that you want to have. You must rely on yourself to be the one who cultivates the love you want to experience and generate the joy you want to feel. You must build your loving and joyful home within yourself, not within others.

HE LOST HIMSELF IN HER

Following him up the steps to his bedroom, I noticed that this wasn't going to be a normal conversation that my good friend and I were about to have. Sitting down on his bed across from him, I noticed right away that something was going on and something wasn't right.

As we looked into each other's eyes, what I saw worried me. For what I saw was a familiar sight that I was to used to seeing. Sitting across from him, I not only saw a young kid whose eyes were screaming for help, but I also saw a reflection of my suffering self in him. The reflection of my suffering self-intensified as I continued to look into his eyes and felt what he was feeling, and my heart began to ache.

As my heart began to sink into my gut, I knew right then and there, that I had to show him that my eyes were the eyes of hope, faith, love and guidance. For I knew exactly what was going on all too well and I knew that he needed me to be fully present with him. Minutes had gone by before a word was spoken. As soon as he began to say a few words, he cried until the tears from a broken heart were flowing down his cheeks. I knew right away what was happening, for I knew those tears and that aching sound of not being able to grasp a breath of air because your heart is in so much pain.

I sat there letting him know that I was there for him as he cried, until he finally said to me, "Tyler, I am lost, broken and my heart is extremely hurt. My girlfriend and I just broke up and I feel as though I've lost everything. My identity, my love, my heart and myself." What I heard when he spoke those words, was a heart screaming for a sense of purpose, and a mind seeking for a clean and clear vision that would make him feel triumphant and excited about life again.

What I saw in those moments of watching and listening to my best friend suffer, was a young man who no longer had a positive relationship with himself. It was rather hard for me to sit there knowing that I couldn't take the pain away. That was all I wanted to do. It broke my heart knowing that this break up was tearing him apart inside and causing him to feel so lost, broken and hopeless.

As I sat there, trying to figure out how I could make him remember his worth and how much he is loved, I found myself lost in my own thoughts. I guess it was his heartbreak that triggered my old pain and heartbreak.

As old feelings crept into my heart and mind, I remembered my own break up and remembered how a break up with your significant other can do this to you. It can make you feel lost, scared, hopeless and worthless. As he went on to express himself and how he was feeling, he kept saying how lost and broken he was.

The thought of feeling lost is just another way of saying, "I no longer have a vision or know who I am", like so many of us out there in this crazy world, right after we lose our significant other or something that we have grown attached to.

Many of us have felt that same empty feeling that my friend was expressing to me, which leaves us lost in the wilderness with no map showing us how to get back home to the place where love, joy, and excitement are flowing through our veins making us feel alive.

My best friend was the one who, after his break up, found himself cast out into the wilderness without the map to bring him back home to the feeling of love and peace. He was the one who had two eyes that could see what had happened and a heart that could feel the separation.

However, what he did not have was the road map that would help him find his way back to love. He was lost without a deep understanding of who he was or who he could be without her. He didn't know how to feel, how to act, who he wanted to be, or where he wanted to take his life after this troubling event, so he stayed in the wilderness within his mind and suffered for many more weeks and months to come.

All this pain, confusion, sadness, and frustration that he continued to feel all became a part of who he was because he built his home within her. Building his home within her caused him to lose himself and when she finally left him, who he thought he was, left with her.

She left him with a broken heart that experienced a sense of nothingness, a lack of excitement, a lack of purpose, hopelessness, isolation, lost and confusion. The perfect place to begin again, as I would like to say. You see, losing yourself after a break up is the best way to find yourself all over again. Often, it's the perfect time to rebuild your home within yourself and become the person who you were always meant to be.

Losing your significant other isn't the hard part. The hard part is losing your identity following the break-up. The hard part is not losing your partner, it's who you were with them that you think you can no longer be.

Dealing with your feelings, following a tragedy, is one of the toughest things will do. No one wants to face themselves alone. Facing yourself alone is a hard battle to win. That's why I think everyone runs to someone while they are facing a break up, divorce, death, or whatever it may be that they consider a tragedy.

I was one of those people. I couldn't stand the thought of being alone because I didn't know or remember who I truly was after my break up. Trying to figure out why it was so hard to be alone, I stumbled upon a rather important discovery. What I've discovered was that in many relationships, many of us build our homes inside of our significant other's rather than building our home within ourselves. We lose ourselves in others.

The truth is, we build our love and identity in that person, and we expect them to stay with us and make us happy. However, this is never a good idea! What we should do, instead of building a home within them, is build our own home within ourselves.

This is what we need to work on. A home that has a powerful and loving foundation that can empower us to live a greater quality of life and get through tough times even when life crashes down around us. When everything in our life falls apart, many of us fall apart with it. This fall is often experienced when we lose our significant other or something that we have attached ourselves to.

I've also found that sometimes some of us fall so far, that we find ourselves being a person whom we no longer can recognize. We become the type of person who only sees the darkness that is taking over inside of us, rather than seeing the true blessing behind the tragedy. That is how my good friend and I felt. We became the person who lived within a suffering mindset, which destroyed the self-worth and self-love that we once had toward ourselves.

Have you ever found yourself in this same type of suffering mindset before? Where you just feel as if you are being consumed by a life full of darkness and negativity? I am sure many of you have. And if you have or are living there right now, I want you to deeply know and accept this truth; this too shall pass, and the best is yet to come.

Stay hopeful and strong. For this is meant to strengthen you, not break you. This is supposed to break you so allow it to happen so that you can rebuild a new you. A new you that you are going to love to be, a new you who you were always meant to be.

Many before you have made it through these dark and tough times and you can do the same. Stay committed to loving who you are and who you are becoming. Don't be so hard on yourself. Be patient with this and what you are going through because a brighter tomorrow is on its way.

Those are the words of affirmation I remember myself saying to myself every day. I needed these words of affirmations to get me through this brokenness and fear of never being able to heal and finally feel back to normal. These daily words were powerful reminders that helped me get through the time where all I could do is rely on others to make me feel happier, safe, cared for and loved. They were the foundation to my personal success. Those were the words that kick-started my healing process and are what helped me to build a powerful and loving relationship with myself.

IT WAS TIME TO HEAL

I got to the point where I became so fed up of relying on others to heal me and bring me happiness, that I knew it was time to take matters into my own hands and begin to do some deep healing. Until the broken come to complete terms with the fact that it is, they themselves who have been the authors of their own misfortune, and until they realize it's up to them to alter the course of their own lives, they are doomed and will not heal.

Relying on someone to bring you happiness and love isn't something you should do. For what I found would happen, not only to myself, but to everyone who did this, is that everything that we believed we were when we were with them, ends up being demolished by a massive wrecking ball which crushes our heart and identity when they leave. That's what happens when loss occurs.

That's what happened to my friend, and why, when he lost his significant other, he not only lost her, but he lost himself, along with his happiness, love, purpose, and identity. **While losing yourself is one of the worst feelings some of us may ever feel, the only way to keep yourself from losing yourself, is by not allowing yourself to build your home or identity within another person**.

Losing your identity is never easy, and you can save yourself from the pain by building a stronger home within yourself. The home within yourself should be a home where you feel free to authentically express yourself and feel love constantly flowing in like a gentle summer breeze. For if you begin to work on you and understand what you bring to the table, you will never be afraid to eat alone. You can rely on yourself to bring you back to peace, love and joy when struggle and turmoil occur. You can experience a beautiful and strong relationship with yourself and others once you learn that your happiness and love should never be given to another.

Let me clarify what I just stated. You should never make it another person's responsibility to make you feel happy and loved. Yes, they can contribute to the love and joy you experience, but you should never make them fully responsible for supplying you with the goods. You need to hold yourself responsible for supplying yourself with the goods that consist of peace, joy, love and light. You can give them your happiness and love, but you should not give it to them and then rely on them to give it to you.

The goods should be constantly generated within you so that when something happens, like a break up, a death or some other form of loss, you don't lose yourselves completely and end up in a dark place. It's hard to climb out of that dark place and rough storms once you're in them. However, as long as you remember to cultivate and generate love and joy within yourself first, you will no longer have to worry about your well-being when lightning decides to strike.

Being able to cultivate and generate what you want to experience in your life will help you be able to not worry so much and allow yourself to become more vulnerable and open to living a fuller life.

Lightening can and will strike anyone of us at any time in our life. It can strike our heart and make us feel lost, depressed, lonely, disconnected and hopeless. But by understanding that you can create an unshakable home or identity, you will be on your way to experiencing real and powerful relationships with yourself, others and God, which will then allow you to experience your fullest life.

This is a beautiful life, and it is a life in which you will travel with yourself for the entire time. You are not going anywhere so I suggest you get to building a powerful and loving relationship with yourself so that you can enjoy life and the power of creating loving relationships with others. You are the key that will unlock a life worth living, and more importantly, a life worth remembering.

You are the key that will unlock your own joy and love when you decide you are ready. All you have to do is commit and begin working on the relationship you have with yourself. You already know deep within you what your heart and soul need, so just do what you know deep within you to be true. Do the work that needs to be done. Although, it might be hard to face yourself, it is going to be well worth it.

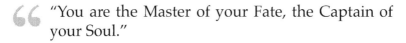 "You are the Master of your Fate, the Captain of your Soul."

— HENRY FORD.

It's in your hands now to begin to craft the masterpiece you were always meant to be. You truly are the master of your own reality and the captain of your inner world. Begin creating the person you want to become by focusing on generating beautiful images on the screen of your mind.

Picture what it would be like to experience your own joy, your own love, your own light, and your own unique energy within yourself. Brendon Burchard once made a very powerful statement in one of his podcast episodes on The Brendon Show. He said, "The power plant doesn't just have energy; it transforms one form to another. It generates energy and transmits it. We are the same. You don't have happiness, you generate it. I say if you are going to generate any form of energy let it be joy and love. Let that be your intention, and the lights will come on and shine through you."

I carry this statement with me every day. You truly do have the ability to generate a powerful and loving relationship within yourself. Believe it! Accept it! Be it! God has given you the gift to create and generate the life, relationships, love, joy, and success you have always deserved.

You must find it within yourself to fully accept this to be true and more importantly get to know thyself on a deeper level. You must begin to reevaluate your present moment and reexamine your future goals. Begin right now, look straight ahead and fill your mind with beautiful and grand thoughts of what you ultimately could do and what you eventually can be.

You have the power to change your reality by changing where you focus your thoughts. If you can truly believe this, you will be able to build the relationship you have always wanted to have with yourself and become the person you always knew you could be. You will be able to generate a greater sense of self-worth, self-love, and full acceptance. You will always have the deep inner confidence that no matter what the storm may bring, you can and will get through it.

That is a lesson which you must take home with you. For the truth of the matter is, your home is only as happy, joyful and loving as you allow it to be. You are the one who is in control of what you are going to generate within your mind and how you are going to feel. So why feel and be anything less than love, joy, excitement, and a vibrant light that bursts from you no matter where you are?

Make your home one that is full of light and love, that shines through every window, and with the doors wide open to allow anyone in who may need your help. You are the creator of your own reality. You are the captain of your own soul. You are the demon lurking in every dark corner, and you are the light in every star.

With this knowledge and with that power, I ask that you go out there and be the torch that radiates loving energy in a room that is filled with so much darkness. You can be the one who brings love, hope and joy into the lives of all those who are in need of it. For you will never be forgotten when you are the person who is the light in the darkness for another.

There are many others out there standing in the dark feeling alone and lost. Show them the way. Be the way. Have faith that you are the way. You will always have it in you. But it's up to you to decide whether or not you want to live in a house strong enough to withstand the storms.

Come with me today, and let it be our commitment to go out into this world, put our best foot forward, and live inside of our own stone castles. If you want a house of stone, built on a strong foundation that will withstand any heartbreak, all you have to do is know who you are and understand who you want to be. Get super clear on this. Then focus all your attention on creating that person and live every day being aware of who you are today and who you will become tomorrow. This will help you be the light and love you need to be for yourself.

5

A LOVING VISION

"A man without a vision is a man without a future. A man without a future will always return to his past."

— P.K. Bernard

How many of you out there currently lack a vision for yourself and for your life? How many of you out there find yourself being haunted by your past, only to find that you're being pestered and hurt on a regular basis? How many of you out there let your past effect your current mood or your current relationship with yourself, with others and with God?

For many years, I let my past define me and haunt me, which led to a ruined relationship with myself. I allowed my broken home to make me feel broken inside. I allowed my break ups to make me feel unworthy of love. I allowed my inability to get into the division one college I wanted, to define me as a failure. I allowed my inability to read, write and do math make me feel less than all my classmates. I allowed my fear of losing someone never allow me to fully open myself up to anyone.

I let my bullies, who would always call me gay, make fun of me and who always wanted to fight me, dictate the quality of life I would live throughout my childhood years. I let so much from my past bring me down to the ground and define me as a person who didn't allow happiness or love into his life.

That was until I had enough of it all and began to let go of my past pains and push forward to create a new vision for myself and my life. You will never obtain any substantial measure of personal joy or fulfillment if you insist upon living your life as if you were looking back through the rearview mirror of your automobile.

Knowing what needed to be done but unsure how to get it done was when I started to look for the teachers and book to learn the lessons that could teach me to live a better quality of life. This was the time in my life where I learned from powerful people like Tony Robbins, Bob Proctor, Dr. Wayne W. Dyer, Lewis Howes, Brendon Burchard and T. D. Jakes. All of these great teachers have helped me focus in on the power of a clear and specific vision and learn how a vision would help me power up my life like I've never known possible.

After spending many hours with these guys through podcasting, seminars, books and YouTube videos, I understood how to build the vision that would help me overcome the negative relationship I had with myself and others in my life. I learned that your vision will help you stick to your 'true north' when you are feeling lost. It will help you find clarity when it comes time to figure out what you will say "yes" to and accept and what you will say "no" to.

Your ability to say yes and no is what will keep you on your true north and allow you to feel truer to yourself. It will help you overcome all the negativity and stay more focused on the positivity. Building your vision for who you want to be and how you want your life to turn out will help you be truer to who you are and who you want to become. Your vision is the bridge between your present and your future. Without your vision, you will perish and allow life to control you, rather than allowing yourself and God to control your life. **When it comes to building this relationship with yourself, it is very important to have your vision in sight at all times, for it will give your pain a purpose and allow you to overcome struggle a lot easier**.

For those of you who don't have a vision, life will seem as though it is working against you a lot more often. It will seem as if your internal pain will drag on a lot longer and reoccur a lot more often. That is why those without a vision to chase, go through life feeling victimized and less fortunate than their peers.

You will find that many of those who don't have a vision run away from their pain rather than face it. For those with a vision know that their pain is trying to tell them something and help them transform into their better selves and get back on their true north. Without a vision and by trying to avoid the everyday struggle life tries throws at you, you begin to avoid the life you were supposed to live and the person you were supposed to become.

However, if you have a vision for yourself and your life, the pain will begin to empower you to evolve into your best self. Learning to accept the pain, by allowing my vision to overcome my struggle, helped me to grow into my better self. It helped me to understand that this pain is temporary, and I am not my pain but the observer to the pain.

It has helped me to know that this internal pain that I was dealing with would pass. For many years I was a kid who lacked personal purpose, love, and a vision. And because of this, I would always adapt my parents and friends' situations and problems as my own. Always finding myself in struggling situations, I felt like my life was doomed from the get-go. For I never had any clear direction as a kid. As I grew older and a little bit wiser, I believe I started to realize the power of separation.

Throughout the many separations I had experienced growing up, what I came to realize at the end of my senior year in high school, was that other people's problems and situations were not mine to own, and they only become so when I made them. And the only time that you and I make these problems ours, is when we lack a vision that helps us realize what is actually ours and what is actually theirs.

Many of you out there right now are lacking vision and attaching yourself to other people's visions and problems. This is an issue that is only doing you more harm than good. For all you are doing is attaching yourself to another's dream and life, so that you can avoid the pain and work it takes to live your own life.

Part of the process of developing a powerful and loving relationship with yourself, others and the Divine, is you must decide what you want in life and stop playing around. It's the only life you have. Create it. Visualize it. Be it. Live it. Enjoy it. Make it a great one.

Many of you out there are doing the exact opposite of figuring out what you want in life and who you want to become. For when it comes time to figuring out your vision and what it is you really want, you stop short because of the "I don't know" phrase. This is a phrase that suppresses your power in so many ugly ways or you are someone who doesn't feel the aliveness that today has in store for you, so you pick up your phone looking for life.

You see, many of us today, spend so much of our lives doing all of these random things to avoid the truth, the pain, ourselves, and our lives, all because we are too afraid to push ourselves and to feel the growth pains that come with growing into our best selves. Too many of us are spending too much of our lives doing the tasks that we are told to do rather than doing the tasks that are meaningful and purposeful to our life's work and vision and who we want to see ourselves as.

I am not saying that doing what we are told to do is a bad thing. However, way too many people are becoming too distracted by the things that others want us to do and are not truly stepping into our own greatness or embracing the wonderful opportunities that life has granted us. The life that has been given and gifted to you, is yours to create.

If you have not yet taken control of your wonderful gift of life, then consider yourself a drifter. A drifter is someone who sits around and just coasts through life, never really deciding what they want out of life or who they want to be. They are the ones who never generate the feelings they want to feel and evolve into the person they were supposed to be.

As a drifter, many random things start to happen to you in your life. As these random things begin to happen, the drifter sees them as issues and begins to identify with those issues. They let their issues define them instead of building them. Don't allow your issues to stop you from becoming the person you were meant to be.

Create the vision of who you want to be and start taking small steps towards becoming that confident and loving person, so that when the day comes and tragedy strikes, and the storms of the sea seem monstrous, you are ready to become the captain of your ship and are able to navigate your way through the storm and be on your true path.

Don't be a drifter and watch your life go by. Become the captain of your ship and realize that these storms that strike you are only there to help you get on your own specific path. Allow your vision to reveal your true north and let the storm strengthen you.

As you set your sail and venture out into the deep blue sea, trying to find who you truly are and build a powerful and loving relationship with yourself, be aware of the problems that may stop you from developing your vision for a wonderful life.

The number one reason why you may not find a vision for yourself, is because you just might not believe that you can achieve and be whatever it is you want to be in your life. Don't allow this to stop you. You must recognize the underlying beliefs that are playing against you and come to acknowledge what you are saying to yourself while you are trying to go after your fullest life; one that is full of joy, love, health, wealth and powerful relationships.

What you may say to yourself is "I am not good enough and I can't have a great and loving relationship." Or, "I can't have the body that I want so I can't be happy." **Anything you cannot confront, you will not be able to conquer. To conquer it, you have to confront it**. I am asking you to confront your negative thoughts, emotions, and beliefs that run through your mind. I ask you to confront them so you can conquer them. As thoughts of negativity rush through your mind, you must reconnect to who you want to become and push through the thoughts that will keep you from achieving the relationships you want and having the life you deserve.

As I stumbled upon these disempowering thoughts, emotions, and beliefs, I realized just how much I wanted to quit and give up, and not progress towards my vision. I allowed those three internal pieces to control the quality of life I lived and the relationship I had with myself, others, and God. You may find yourself in the same boat, just as many others do.

But this time you know the secret that will help you get over these internal hurdles that you will face. You now know what I did to overcome these disempowering beliefs, emotions, and thoughts so that I could have the confidence and courage to chase my dreams, write this book, and build powerful and loving relationships with myself, others, and God.

My secret to gaining this wonderful internal success that consists of joy, love and fulfillment is to create your vision, stick to your vision and more importantly, stay true to your word. Because when you have a powerful and clear vision and stick to your word, you will find it easier to reconnect yourself to your vision and fight your way through the internal and external storms that await us all.

You must learn to prevail and take back your thoughts by focusing on your visions. I promise you, if you are someone who does not create a vision for themselves when carrying around these thoughts in your mind, you will find it a lot harder to prevail and become the person you want to be and have the life you want to live with those whom you love the most.

When sailing on your boat of life, without a strong enough vision to carry you through the stormy seas, you will find yourself wanting to give up, for you have nothing to hold on to and push you and keep you from not wanting to give up. You will be so caught up in self-sabotage while facing those tough times, that you will lose a lot of your willpower to keep moving yourself forward.

You will realize that all of these massive waves of "I can't", that you have been getting hit with, will cause your boat to roll and become your reality You will soon find yourself under the sea fighting for another breath. Your words will find a way into your life to make sure that what you say, will happen in your life. You find a way to make yourself right. That is why you must have a clear and powerful vision. So that when these waves of "I can't" or "I am not good enough" do strike you, they don't overcome you nor do they become you.

But let it be known, when you do find yourself in the seas of hell, beating yourself up and thinking negatively, always remember that you are not alone. For God is with you and within you battling against the same stormy seas. Everyone goes through their stormy seas while chasing after their best self and making their vision become a reality. However, understand that during those times, you must decide which thoughts you are going to listen to. And with the help of a clear vision, you will be able to find those powerful thoughts and follow them through the storm.

You must decide that who you want to be, what you want to have, what you want to create and how you want to live, is everything you can have. Just like the great William Arthur Ward once said, "If you can imagine it, you can achieve it. If you can dream it, you can become it." So, empower yourself with a vision and write down the three words you want to live and become. Make it your mission to live those three words and that vision out daily.

6

FINDING YOURSELF

> "Finding yourself is not really how it works. You aren't a ten-dollar bill in last winter's coat pocket. You are also not lost. Your true self is right there, buried under cultural conditioning, other people's opinions, and inaccurate conclusions you drew as a kid that became your beliefs about who you are. Finding yourself is actually returning to yourself. An unlearning, an excavation, a remembering who you were before the world got its hands on you."
>
> — EMILY McDOWELL

Going back to seventh grade, when I felt like doing everything I could to run away from the person who my heart was telling me I was, I found myself making a life-changing decision that helped me to cope with the heartbreak and past that I was holding on to. I tried to hide the pain and my past in any way that I could. Seventh grade was the year that I really started to run away from my thoughts, feelings and upbringing. I looked for different ways to cope with my internal suffering.

With the help of my brother, I decided to get myself into the gym and work on becoming that "one-day" senior running back that dominated the field. For five years I would find myself using my internal pain to push me through my external pain. After five years without missing more than a week in the gym, I started to build a bigger and more powerful me. One who could easily fool others into believing that everything was okay, and that I was a man. I built a self that could not only dominate the football field but also dominate the emotional outrage that I felt on a daily basis.

However, the weight room was only a temporary fix to my internal suffering. It never seemed to completely heal the past pain, it only became one of the ways in which I would deal with the hurt and suppress it. I hated suppressing who I was and how I felt on the inside. I hated it because it made me feel so trapped in my own skin. For the truth be told that behind the muscles and the figure I created, was a broken child, ashamed to cry, ashamed to love, and ashamed to feel anything but the pain.

It wasn't until I finally graduated from high school, and was put out on my own, that I found my true self, deep behind the image I created. **Finding the real you behind the person you created, so that you no longer have to suppress your authentic self, is like trying to find a needle in a haystack.**

You must really learn how to let go and accept your pain and your scars. Behind each one of your unique scars, you will find something so beautiful, it just might make you cry and open your heart. You just might find the person you were always meant to be. Deep behind my suffering was the real me. Deep behind my broken heart, was the me that my heart knew I was all along. Behind the fake me was the real me, who I always wanted to be, but was too afraid to be.

For in a man's world, it was weak of me to be the man who my heart wanted me to be, or so I thought. However, as I kept learning more about myself and how to deal with my internal world and scars, I began to find something amazing. What I found behind my scars was a young man who knew that love was everything.

I found a man who enjoys loving, leading and serving others into a better quality of life. I found a man who loves to cry. I found a man who enjoys being vulnerable and being himself. I found a man who loves to be hugged, and a man who loves to express joy into the hearts of others. I found a man who cares so deeply about other people, that he has now made it his life's mission to help people build powerful and loving relationships with themselves, others and the Divine, so that they can start living their best life.

I found a man who was made out of love and whose mission it was to help others love themselves, others, and God more openly. Without judgement. Once I let go of the old me and allowed myself to just be me, I learned that I am a man full of love and empathy, joy and excitement. Now, just because I have learned what type of man I am, doesn't mean these things that I know I am come easy to me.

Being loving, joyful, courageous, kind and confident are a struggle for me at times. Finding a gentle and loving man at the depths of my being scared me, for it broke all of my original beliefs of what it means to be a man. But who I found and who I am deep down made me feel more alive and authentic.

Getting to know yourself on a deeper level by connecting to your heart will open the doors that will help you to unlock your personal freedom. I hope you understand what awaits you when you learn to give yourself the permission you need in order to be the person you have always wanted to be and have the things you want and deserve. You must learn, as I have learned, to let go and accept the person you think you are and realize that the real you is behind the person which you have created to protect your heart.

For when you let go of the person you are for others, and accept that the person that you have built is the person you are not, then you will have allowed yourself permission to actually become the person you were meant to be. This will allow you to have the best loving relationship you deserve to have with yourself. 'Being you and not hiding behind the image you created yourself to be for the sake of others, is such a freeing feeling. Giving yourself the permission needed to actually do whatever it is you truly want to do, be who you want to be, and build what you want to build, is something you must learn to do, for who you truly are relies upon it.

I know that this may sound simple, but please don't overlook this. **Give yourself the permission needed to actually want what your heart truly wants**. I know how crazy this might sound right now, because it all starts with allowing yourself to actually want to open up your heart and your true self to the world.

However, giving yourself permission to be vulnerable, is the key that will unlock your fullest life. It's the key that will open up your heart to allow yourself to love you again. The reason you might find it hard to love yourself is because you are not being who you know you truly are supposed to be.

Too many people suppress their true selves and only allow themselves to be half of what they truly can be. It's hard to love and accept yourself when you are not being yourself. They believe that they can only have an average life and relationship with themselves.

You see, many of us believe we can have the average relationship or the average car because it's what is normal, and it's what most people have and do. However, this isn't the reason why you were born. You were not born to shelter your true self from the world or be an average cookie cutter person.

God didn't create you to not chase your dreams, be you aren't meant to be or have an average relationship with yourself, others, and God. You were created by the highest God to have everything you have ever envisioned and dreamed up, to be the person you have always dreamed of being and to have powerful and loving relationships with The Big Three. You can be who you were meant to be as long as you deeply accept you as you are on the deepest of levels. You are in the deepest of all levels of love. Love is who you are and what you are at the deepest of levels.

As soon as you deeply accept this truth, your life will begin to dramatically change for the greater good. However, as soon as you believe that something like love is out of your reach, right then and there, it becomes off limits to you. That is why you have to give yourself permission to want what your heart really wants. All your heart wants is love. It wants to give love, be loved, and receive love. For you deserve to have what you have always wanted, I hope you know that and believe that.

Whilst on the pursuit of your wildest dreams, whether you're in the process of moving toward a relationship you want to have, obtaining a car, or achieving a bank account number, they can seem impossible to get to. But what you will receive at the end of the journey will make it worth it. All because you are trying to achieve that thing you gave yourself permission to achieve.

The person that you become during the pursuit, after you give yourself permission, is really the greatest gift. While you are on your pursuit, all you must do is decide what it is you really want, and then move in that direction. I am here with you! We are in this together! Give yourself permission and watch the floodgates open up to more self-worth, self-compassion, self-support and self-love.

Here are the steps that I told my good buddy to take in order to get him out of the thoughts and emotions that were destroying him deep down inside. We heal and get through life's most difficult challenges when we learn to set the intention and create a clear vision, visualize our dream of our best self, be intentional every day to be that person you visualize, and finally, love yourself more. So, let's make sure you are clear on who it is you want to be and what it is you truly want. Below, you'll walk through what your powerful and loving relationship with yourself will look like.

As I sat down in front of him that night, I asked God to help me through it. I asked that he open my heart and my mind and let my words connect to my friend's heart. I asked God to help me uncover the many lessons I had learned throughout my past, and to help him get through life's toughest challenges. And what I heard myself telling him were a few discoveries I had made which we can all benefit from. In order to get your life back, and to progress forward successfully after any challenge, you must first create a clear and specific vision that will bring you hope and catch your soul on fire.

EXERCISE: CREATE YOUR POWER VISION

 "The more clarity you achieve, the more you will find that the universe is on your side, supporting your thoughts and intentions. Therefore, focus on clarity, not on getting results. The results will come according to their own rhythm and timing."

— DEEPAK CHOPRA

The first part of this vision exercise will help you get a clear understanding of what you want and who you want to become. In order to invite love into your life, we need to first ask ourselves some very important personal questions:

1. Who am I?
2. What do I stand for?
3. What are my values?
4. What are my truths?
5. Which truths no longer serve me?
6. Which truths serve me?
7. What is my vision for myself, for others and for this world?
8. Who do I want to be in a year from now?
9. How can I start being who I want to be, in a year from now, today?
10. How do I want to feel every day? List three main feelings that I would like to experience.
11. What does my best version of myself look and feel like?
12. At the end of my life, what are the three to five things I want to be remembered for?
13. At the end of my life, what are the three to five things I want people to say about me?

7

VISUALIZATION

> "If you have a clear picture in your head that something is going to happen and a clear belief in that, it will happen, no matter what, then nothing can stop it, it is destined to happen and that's what happens. It's perfect."
>
> — CONOR McGREGOR

After you answer the questions, the next step to living the life you want is to visualize who it is you want to be. The goal is to not only see it in your mind's eye but feel like you are already that person. Choose the vision that feels good and practice seeing that vision every day until you own it, until you are it and become it.

You see, one of the greatest secrets to life is that the more you visualize and focus on what it is you want, who you want to be and how you want to feel, every subject must then rise to meet you there. In other words, what you focus on will grow and become one with you. Who you want to be and what you want to have can all become possible as soon as you begin to visualize it and feel what it would be like to have it.

Throughout my many years of studying the top performers out there, regardless of what profession they are in, I have learned that they all know this one true lesson and exercise: They understand the importance of picturing yourself being your best self and succeeding in your mind's eye before you actually do it in reality. This is one of the most important lessons and exercises you will ever do for yourself.

Once I began to understand that this is what all the world's best athletes, entrepreneurs, singers, dancers, teachers and world changers are doing, I began to implement it. I studied to understand the power of visualization; I started to recognize that the many successful people who did visualize a better life and worked hard, experienced the outcome they saw in their mind's eye.

I have learned that this practice has been one of the keys that unlock the great success that many high achievers use daily, and that has helped them unlock their dreams by staying focused on what it is they truly want. There are so many powerful and real examples out there of many people who use visualization and The Law of Attraction to help them get what they desire and be who they desire to become. I recommend you use them and do the same.

One of my favorite actors of all time talked about it on the Oprah Winfrey Show. Jim Carrey often speaks publicly about his strong belief in the Law of Attraction and visualization. Jim is most well-known for his interview with Oprah, where he explains his process of visualization and The Law of Attraction.

On the show, Jim described his process about how he used the power of intention and visualization to achieve his success in the film industry and earned his first ten million dollars. In this interview Jim stated, "As far as I can tell, it's just about letting the universe know what you want and then working toward it while letting go of how it comes to pass." Now that is some great advice from one of the greatest and funniest actors of all time! If you can truly understand and implement this advice into your own life, you can create the life, freedom, love, and success your heart truly desires.

FIVE TIPS FOR CREATING YOUR REALITY

To help you out a little bit more, I want to describe to you the five tips that Jim Carrey used to help create the reality that his heart desired.

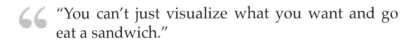 "You can't just visualize what you want and go eat a sandwich."

— JIM CARREY

To create the reality that your heart truly desires, you can't just visualize what it is you want and go play video games, watch Netflix, go out and party or whatever else you may enjoy doing with your free time. To create the reality that your heart truly desires, it's going to take massive action. You must take massive action! One of my favorite YouTubers of all time, Casey Neistat has said it best, "Until we put some action behind the intention, the intention will always just be a dream." You must not just visualize what it is you want and who you want to be, you must act on it! The Law of Attraction will not work without action!

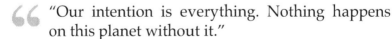 "Our intention is everything. Nothing happens on this planet without it."

— JIM CARREY

The intention that you set daily is the foundation for how

your life will turn out that day. You create your own reality. Every event that takes place, every experience you go through are all your creations. You are the great creator. The one who creates everything through your intentions you set and desires you hold in your heart. No matter the experience you are going through in your life, you were the one to create that experience. Whether it's the most beautiful experience of your life or the crappiest day of your life, you are the creator. In every moment, live fully present, and ask yourself "What do I really want to create today?" Allow this question to move into the depths of your heart. Find your answer there.

 "You can ask the Universe for it."

— JIM CARREY

Nothing is out of reach. Everything is within your grasp; you just have to ask for it. There is nothing in this world that is too big or too small. You will be the only person who stops yourself from becoming the person you want to become and having the life you want to live. Don't be afraid of your deepest desires. Don't allow fear to settle into your heart and stop you from asking what it is it wants. Don't limit yourself from asking for everything your heart desires.

 "As far as I can tell, it's just about letting the Universe know what you want and working toward it, while letting go of how it comes to pass."

— JIM CARREY

When it comes to becoming who you want to be and having the relationships you want to have, there is nothing you need to control. If you want to find that special someone, fall in love, and get married, you don't need to decide how every date night is going to go or what every text message will say. You just need to work toward your greatest desire of getting married and having a beautiful family, while letting the Universe decide how you'll get there. The more you allow yourself permission to let go and have faith that God has your back, the better chance you will end up right where you need to be.

> "I believe in manifestation," says Carrey. "I believe in putting a rocket of desire out into the Universe. And you get it when you believe it."
>
> — JIM CARREY

There is an old saying out there that says, "Seeing is believing." However, when it comes to creating the relationship you want or having the things you desire the most, the Law of Attraction works a bit differently. You see, the Law of Attraction states that believing is seeing. Once you truly believe in something, then you'll actually see it materialize in your reality. You can spend endless hours visualizing, reciting your affirmation, or making your lists of all the things you want. But as Jim Carrey points out, it's when you believe it that you'll get it.

There are so many other great examples of those who follow what I have taught you and what Jim Carrey has taught many of us. For example: Boxing legend, Muhammad Ali, was always expressing the importance of seeing himself victorious long before the fight would take place. Michael Jordan is another who always used this to visualize his last shot in his mind before he ever took the shot in reality.

There are so many other top performers and world-class entrepreneurs out there who have used this technique to get them out of the suffering life they once lived, to where they are today. In fact, many of the people who I look up to like Shawn Stevenson, Lewis Howes, Bob Proctor, Tony Robbins and Oprah Winfrey, have all used the technique of positive visualization. They have been very open about how powerful it is and how it is an important success tactic to be used daily. The best part about this technique is that we all have this amazing ability within us. You have the special gift within you right now to visualize your best life.

However, the problem most of us have is that many of us have never been taught how to use it effectively. That is why I am going to offer you my daily practice of visualization that has helped me accomplish my dreams and write this book. I have also been able to help other great athletes, the wealthy, and many peak performers in all fields, accomplish their dreams and goals.

Below is a step-by-step guide that will help you achieve your desired outcomes. This step-by-step process will walk you through what your powerful and loving relationship with yourself will look like and feel like. (Note: you can use this concept with more than just your relationship.) You see, visualization is rather easy to do. A lot easier than you might think.

What seems to help me get into a state of visualization, and what can also help you, is to first find a comfortable position. You can either sit or lie down flat on your back. I normally lie down. Then close your eyes gently and start the imagination process. This is where your thoughts will become very vivid and you will visualize in great detail what your life would be like if you were the person you always dreamed of becoming. I personally set aside about ten minutes on a daily basis, right when I wake up or after I meditate. I have found that the best times are when you first wake up or right before you go to bed.

These are the times we are most relaxed and in our alpha brain wave state of mind. These alpha brain waves are created when we are truly relaxed. When you get into the alpha brain wave frequency, you are normally in the meditative state. When activated, your brain wave frequency will heighten your imagination, visualization, memory, learning, and concentration. This is the gateway to the subconscious mind and will help you with many important things.

Here is the seven-step process that I go through for ten minutes each morning, which helps me visualize a better quality of life and relationship with myself:

EXERCISE: SEVEN-STEP PROCESS

Step #1: Close your eyes and pretend you are watching a movie of the life that you have always wanted to live and the person you have always wanted to be. Visualize and imagine yourself sitting in your own movie theater. Find yourself letting go of all of today's worries and problems and just relax your entire body. Relax everything. You can relax everything by taking a deep breath in, breathing into your lower gut for five seconds, holding it for five seconds, then breathing out for five seconds, and holding again for five seconds. Do these three to five times in succession.

Step #2: Shift your focus from your breath to your body. While still breathing, start to circulate your breath and focus on your toes. Breathe in deeply through your nose if you can, and as you exhale, let your breath travel down to your toes, and then back out, while following the same breathing technique listed in step 1.

Step #3: Take your attention from your toes to your feet by breathing deeply in through your nose for a count of five seconds, hold for five seconds, release for five seconds, and for five seconds, let your breath circulate to your feet. Next, follow the same pattern but move your attention to your ankles, then your shins, then your knees, then your thighs, then into your stomach and lower back, all the way up through your arms, chest, neck, face and to the very top of your head. The objective here is to relax each part of your body, which will help you get into that alpha state of mind.

Step #4: Once you are fully relaxed, imagine yourself back in front of the movie screen and imagine the relationship you want to have with yourself, others, and God. See as much detail and feel as much emotion as you can during this process. Feel what your best life would be like while seeing what it is you want to see. See the clothes you are wearing, the facial expression on your face, the environment and the people who are in your life. See the different types of relationships you will have, the car you will drive, the impact you will have, the character you want to create and play. Add any emotions that will make you feel empowered and excited to go after that life that is awaiting you. Finally, create in your mind, body and feelings what you think you would be experiencing as you are feeling and seeing this amazing life.

Step #5: Once you see and feel your life with an open heart and accepting mind, visualize yourself leaving your comfy chair and walking up to the screen, opening a door and entering into your own movie. Once you enter your movie and embody yourself, look out through your own eyes, and become that best version of yourself. Live in the moment of greatness and feel what it is truly like to be living your fullest life. This activity, in which you become yourself inside yourself, looking out through your eyes, is called an embodied image. This embodied image will deeply affect the experience that you will have, for you will feel as though you are truly there. What your mind can see and believe, it can achieve.

. . .

Step #6: Finally, visualize your journey back out of the movie, and return to your seat in your home theater. Once you are back in your chair, reach out and grab the screen. Once you have the screen in your hands, hold it next to your heart and let it dissolve into it, and imagine it flowing through every cell of your entire body.

Step #7: Once you feel as though you have finished creating your movie of your fullest life, which normally takes me around ten to fifteen minutes, take a deep, full breath in. As you let it out, know that you are sending it off to the Divine, to your God, to the universe or whoever or whatever you may believe in. And believe that what you just visualized is now in the hands of your God, and it is on its way back to you in full force. If you commit this into your daily or even weekly life, and make it a part of your daily routine, you will be truly amazed at how much improvement you will see in your life. Don't look over this. Be disciplined enough to make this a daily or nightly ritual. For I truly believe if you want to become like the best, be seen as the best, and be the best you that you can be, then you must make visualization a part of your daily routine. We must make it as universal as brushing our teeth is to us every morning. I am not here to be average! I am not here to live an ordinary life, generate average feelings, have average thoughts, be the average person who did everyday things, and had a mediocre relationship with myself, my family, my friends, and my God. You and I both were not put on this Earth to be average in our lives. We are here to live an extraordinary life and be exceptional human beings! Bob Proctor said it best when he said, "You are God's highest form of creation! You are a living, breathing creative magnet. You can control what you attract into your life!" This is extraordinary information! This is a powerful truth that can truly change your life! When you understand and take what Bob Proctor said seriously, your life can and will improve exponentially. You can genuinely attract the loving and sincere relationships you want. You can draw the person you want to have in your life. You can attract all the material, spiritual, physical, and emotional wealth you wish to have and experience in your life if you begin the process of visualization!

You were born to be the greatest you that you can be. You are God's highest form of creation! You were born to have extraordinary, sincere, loving, and healthy relationships in your life! Don't miss out on it just because you are too lazy to take matters into your own creative hands and create the life your heart truly desires. You were born because you have an extraordinary experience that awaits you and needs you to show up as your best self to give this world the greatest gift that you can provide it. Your best and authentic self! And the best way that you can begin to step into this extraordinary life and loving relationships is to visualize this remarkable quality of life into existence!

8

SELF-TALK

> " "Perhaps, we should love ourselves so fiercely,
> that when others see us they know exactly how it
> should be done."
>
> — RUDY FRANCISCO

Don't be a victim of discouraging self-talk. You cannot afford to think negative things about yourself if you want to live an extraordinary life and have a great and loving relationship with The Big Three!

Many of us are conscious of the inner voice that provides us with a never-ending monologue throughout our day and typically becomes louder during the nighttime. I know that before practicing meditation, nighttime for me was when my inner critic loved to come out front and center on stage and make itself feel heard.

Speaking over every other voice in my head, it was my inner critic that would find its way to talk so loudly that I could never get it to quieten down or be as positive as I wanted it to be for the longest time. This inner voice caused me to feel like I was never going to be good enough, smart enough, or loved enough. It was this inner voice that created many different internal problems for me as the night began to dwindle, and my head rested upon my pillow. It seemed to me that whenever the lights would turn off, and I would finally get all comfy and cozy in my bed, my inner voice would begin shouting out its opinion on everything. It didn't matter what happened that day.

This inner voice always had a loud and sometimes obnoxious voice. It didn't matter if it was supportive and joyful or negative and self-defeating, this internal chatter wouldn't ever seem to stop, and it's commonly known as self-talk.

Self-talk or your inner voice, combines your conscious thoughts with unconscious beliefs and biases. It's often known as an effective way for your brain to interpret and process daily experiences, which is nice to have when you are standing in line at the grocery store, and someone in front of you is causing all sorts of problems.

This little critic comes in handy when you bite your tongue before you say something you shouldn't to the person at the front of the line causing you to test your patience. Your inner voice is often useful when it is positive, courageous, and joyful, talking down each one of your inner fears and increasing your inner confidence.

However, human nature is prone to deal with negative self-talk and sweeping the "I can't be the person who I want to be" or the "I'm not good enough" assertions under the rug. It is the negative self-talk that has been stopping millions of people from doing what their heart wants them to do and becoming who they want to be.

The reason why most people are not living the life they want to live, with the one they want to live with is because of how they hold a conversation with themselves. You see, if we are unkind to ourselves, it will be challenging to be kind to people for long periods of time. Your true colors will always shine through and eventually show themselves. How you treat yourself is how you will end up treating other people. If you give yourself more love, kindness, and affection, you will show others the same. If you show yourself hate, anger, and frustration, wars and conflicts will begin to take place between you and other people.

Let's calm the conflict by showing ourselves the love we need to experience. It will not be a hard task to accomplish and live out, believe it or not. The relationship you have with yourself can improve each day by the way you talk to yourself. **It is the way you speak to yourself that dictates the quality of life you are going to live that day.** If all you see, hear, and speak is negative, you will only see, hear, chat, and live in that negative relationship with your reality.

However, if you talk to yourself in a loving, confident, and hope-filled way, you will only begin to see the love, hope, and kindness this world truly has to offer and live in that positive relationship with your reality. Take control of your inner voice by becoming more aware of the internal chatter, and you will begin to see quantum shifts in your reality that you have been waiting to experience.

The negative self-talk no longer serves you, those who are around you or humanity. It is this negative self-talk that is causing many of us to live a lower quality of life. It is paralyzing many into inaction and self-absorption to the point of being unaware of the beauty the world and their presence has to offer them. Don't let the small talk cause massive problems in your life. Let it go and allow yourself to forgive yourself for the issues that you create yourself and those around you. This world is overdue for a positive change, and this change can begin to take place the moment we talk more about love in our life.

9

WHAT SELF-LOVE AFFECTS

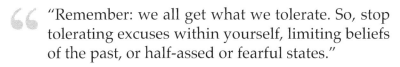

"Remember: we all get what we tolerate. So, stop tolerating excuses within yourself, limiting beliefs of the past, or half-assed or fearful states."

— TONY ROBBINS

How you speak to yourself affects your relationship with yourself, others, and the Divine. It also affects how you see the world and what type of life you are going to live. How you talk, love, and treat yourself, affects how you act and function in your relationships; mainly how you conduct yourself in the relationship you are in, and the standards you uphold for yourself.

I know in my past, I would find myself staying in negative relationships because I didn't have the sense of self-love or self-respect, I needed to do what was right for me. Before I began practicing self-love, I remember being in relationships with those who would only abuse me mentally by lying to me, breaking my heart, calling me names, going behind my back, and so on.

However, I don't blame them for the pain in which I endured. I believe the only reason I put up with that type of relationship behavior and allowed this to happen to me is because I treated myself with the same disrespect. In other words, I only got what I tolerated. I would not allow someone to treat me worse than I would treat myself. I would not be in a relationship that would make me feel worse than I already felt.

However, I would allow myself to be in a broken relationship with another because the relationship with myself was broken. I didn't have a sense of self-love, my standards for what I would allow in my life were shallow, and I had no personal power over my life.

People were able to use me, manipulate me, abuse me, and step all over me, my life, my feelings, my heart, and my mind, as if I didn't matter to them. All because I knew it wasn't as bad as I treated myself, and therefore, I accepted them and the way they treated me.

What I learned as time went on is that if I treated myself with more love and acceptance, I would not accept those hurtful relationships in my life. I would no longer allow those who would treat me worse than I would treat myself in my life.

And at the time, this was a massive lesson that led to the robust and loving relationship breakthrough that I needed. That is one of the reasons why self-love is so important to cultivate in your life. You won't put up with negative, life-draining relationships much longer.

The more self-love you develop and generate in your life, the easier it will be to let go of those who no longer serve you and your best interest. By cultivating self-love, you will be able to ensure that your heart will be taken care of by how you will now be the one in control of how you let others treat you.

You can begin to let go of the negative relationships you have in your life and cultivate a greater sense of self-love by the power of choice. How you react to the relationships you have in your life is something nobody can take from you. You cannot control what happens to you or how people treat you. But you can control your attitude towards what happens to you and how you interrupt how others treat you. In that, you will be able to master your relationships rather than allowing your relationships to master you.

By choosing to love yourself more, you will give yourself a sense of sovereignty, and you will empower yourself to keep the good people in your life who support and love you. You will then have enough courage to remove the bad people who no longer serve you. Something else that I have learned in my studies on self-love, is that it can affect how you take care of yourself.

I know this might sound like a "well, no duh", moment. However, like Brendon Burchard always states, "Common sense is not always common practice, and so we suffer." This is so true! Just because you might know that self-love can affect how you take care of yourself, and help you build a powerful and loving relationship with yourself, it doesn't mean that it is always a common practice to do these certain tasks that will help us love ourselves more.

Practicing self-love can help you enhance the quality of life you live as long as you do what you know will work for you. Self-love is a powerful tool that, when used often, can indeed turn your life around.

You see, self-love isn't about being narcissistic. It's not about "me, me, me." It's not about battling against others, God, or the world to express ourselves or to get what we want. That type of self-love won't get you to have the kind of relationships you want to have in your life. **The self-love I am talking about that many of us need in our lives is about being able to look at yourself in the same way as a loving mother, or a loving God, sees you.**

When you see yourself in the same way that your loving God sees you, love will begin to become very familiar to you, and your heart will start to open. Once your heart fully opens, your true self will start to shine through. The more your true self shines through, the more you will find yourself the person who you have always been meant to be; your sincere, authentic, and loving self.

The love you create for yourself can turn everything around in your life. Once you begin to practice self-love, you will be able to let go of the blame, shame, and anger from the past. You'll be able to take back personal ownership toward the life you are living. You will be able to fully step into your real creative power and be who you were always meant to be. You will be able to take responsibility for your own life. Because at the point you begin to love yourself, you will start to realize that you are the source of all your happiness.

You are the source of the power that can change your present moment around your career, relationship, passion, compassion, confidence, and authenticity. You can generate the love you have always been seeking in the outer world. You hold the internal power.

Now, all that needs to happen to make love settle into your heart and take place in your life is that you must begin to cultivate it and generate it from within. What awaits you on the other side of self-love is a love of the purest of all forms. For the moment you fall in love with yourself is the very moment you fall in love with your creator!

Falling in love with your God will allow you to have the strength, the faith and the courage to let go of loneliness and to be able to embrace a deeper connection and sense of oneness with everything and everyone within the world. The more you look at yourself with love, the more you practice appreciation and acceptance towards others.

On the other side of self-love, you will be able to free yourself. You will no longer be ruled by fear because you will understand that love is the most reliable power of all, and that love is everything. When we choose love over fear, we become stress-free beings open to helping ourselves and others in the greatest of all ways. When we want to love over fear, we all begin to become better lovers, leaders, and servers.

The love you have or do not have for yourself can affect so much in your everyday life. It can affect your work and productivity. It can affect how confident you show up in life. It can affect how punctual you are, how you perform, and in what mindset you complete certain tasks. Your self-love affects all the choices that you make in your life, and it's your choices that will lead you toward your greatest quality of life!

From the big choice of discovering what your purpose in life is going to be, all the way down to the small decision of what you might consume that day. No matter how big or small, self-love affects it all! The way to a better life is to put a dash of love in everything you do.

The more love you put into everything you do, the more you will enjoy everything you do. Your level of self-love will directly affect how you deal with all of your life's greatest challenges. And like I said before, if you learn how to cultivate self-love, you can get through your darkest of hours and courageously seek the proper help you might need.

We can start to enjoy our lives, accept who we are, and live life to the fullest by cultivating a deeper practice of self-love. But before I teach you how you can go about loving and valuing yourself more, so that you can start living your fullest life, I must help you become more aware of the three main enemies that can and will destroy your self-love.

10

SELF-LOVE IS DESTROYED

66 "You will never be able to experience your greatest quality of life until you truly learn to love yourself."

— TYLER JOE STRATTON

I always found it hard to figure out where I went wrong when it came to loving myself. Losing self-love seemed as if it left out of nowhere. It was like one moment I had it, and then before I knew it, it was gone. It became very difficult for me to step outside of myself and truly recognize and reflect on what affects and lowers my self-love.

I found it hard to do because I never gave myself the time I needed to sit back, relax and reflect on my own life. And because of the lack of time I would spend with myself, negative thinking would begin to sneak into my internal world. It was my negative ways of thinking, habits and personal beliefs that lowered my sense of self-love. If you find yourself with the same problems, know we all go through it and it will be okay. **Self-love begins the moment you become aware that love is no longer within**.

After many years of diving deep into myself, learning about what affected and lowered my self-love, I realized that there were many ways in which self-love can be destroyed. However, because there are so many different ways it is destroyed, I will only be covering the three that I believe have the most impact and are most common. These are the three that have caused me, and many more, pain that we don't want to remember.

The lack of love for myself started when I was young. During my elementary school years, is when I began to lose the love that many of us have for ourselves as children. As children, many of us started out having so much self-love and self-compassion flowing through us, to the point that our happiness was the only thing that mattered to us.

All that kids really want is to be happy. So, they focus closely on becoming aware of the things and the people who make them happy. And when something makes them unhappy, they sure do let you know all about it. All we want to do as kids is to be able to do the things which we enjoy and fulfill our hearts. But as we get older and life happens to many of us, this loving and fun nature that is running through us starts to diminish.

I remember when I was in fourth grade; I realized just how different I was from many of my friends. I realized this when we were all outside during recess, playing on our brand-new jungle gym that was just put together. This jungle gym had one of the coolest slides and rock-climbing walls I had ever seen. I was so excited and full of energy as we all ran outside to play on our new jungle gym!

As I was on the top of the slide, about to go down for what felt like the hundredth time, I noticed a teacher that came out to join our class. However, she didn't bring any kids with her. She was standing there next to my fourth grade teacher, talking to her and pointing out a few kids. As she pointed, I noticed that her finger landed right on me. As I slid down the slide, wondering what I had done wrong, my heart stopped.

You see, I wasn't a well-behaved child during those years. I was very rebellious, didn't want to listen. I was always getting kicked off the bus for causing some type of chaos and disruption. Knowing of all the trouble I am used to getting into, I made my way down the slide very slowly, to find my teacher waiting there to greet me with her happy face that was full of care and love.

Her smile had a great effect on my life growing up. It was her smile that would get me through some of my tough days in school. It was my teachers caring smile that made her one of my all-time favorite teachers. However, this time she wasn't my favorite. Once I made my way down the slide, she whispered words into my ear that would haunt me until my eleventh grade year. She went on to whisper, "Tyler, that lady over there is your reading and math tutor and she is here to help you. So, if you could please go inside with her for a little while, that would be wonderful." Wonderful to whom? Not me, that's for darn sure.

From that point on, until my eleventh grade year, I suffered my way through school. Every time I had a moment for myself, I was always with reading, writing or math tutor. It drove me insane. Never being able to have any free time to do what I wanted to do or sit in a study hall caused me to hate going to school even more than I already did.

Always having to leave my friends made me feel so separated and stupid. You see, it was in the fourth grade when I felt this vast separation take place. It was the moment that I began to think that I was not good enough.

When I got home later that day, I questioned what was wrong with me. I compared myself to my friends, and pointed out everything that was wrong with me, from the clothes I was wearing to the funny-looking cowlick I have on the back of my head. That day was the day of a new lousy beginning. A beginning that ended up creating the person who no longer accepted me as me or loved me for who I was.

1: COMPARISON

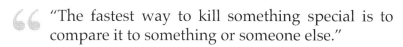 "The fastest way to kill something special is to compare it to something or someone else."

— TYLER JOE STRATTON

Comparing myself to all of those who were having fun, killed my self-love. I deeply believe, with all of my heart, that the first critical blow we take toward our self-love is when we start comparing ourselves to others. My self-love diminished as I kept comparing myself to my friends who were living a better life than me.

On many beautiful days, I was sat at the very end of the school, in a small, sheltered box, being taught how to pronounce words and write sentences. The room had horrible, dim lighting. As I compared myself to my friends, my life became more painful. As the years went by and I kept comparing myself, I only broke myself down even more, feeling worse and worse about everything I was not, and everything I did not have.

Now more than ever, this comparison thing is even more magnified, thanks to the internet and social media. I cannot tell you how many times the internet and social media have caused me to beat myself down for not living as wonderfully as the people who I follow or for getting as many likes as my friends do or building a following as fast as others who I follow.

Can you follow along with what I am saying? Nowadays, all we can see is how everyone around us is living the "dream life". While reflecting on our own lives, we only see how much of our life sucks, and how we don't have that amazing life or that loving relationship like so-and-so does. As we all fall down the pithole of how terrible our lives are compared to others, we only find ourselves with a lower self-worth, self-value, self-esteem, self-compassion and self-love.

We are now in a battle with our everyday life and our ability to care, value, and love ourselves deeply. We seem to have our heads in our phones, being destroyed by every image we scroll over, when our heads should be in the clouds with our God, loving ourselves.

For we are alive and beautiful in our own ways. And it must become our own mission to seek that out in our own selves. Because when you compare yourself to others, what you are really doing is silencing God. I ask that you do not silence God or compare yourselves to others.

For you are unique, beautiful and powerful. See yourself for who and what you truly are. You are a loving and very extraordinary person who is on your own personal journey to unlock your personal freedom, to be who you know you can be and have the life you know you deserve to live.

You must point back to yourself, for there has never been anyone like you before in the history of the world, and there will never be anybody to come who will ever be just like you. You are a gift. You are loved, and you are alive. So, while you are alive, focus on loving your uniqueness more.

2: MORAL FLAW

 "I found I was more confident when I stopped trying to be someone else's definition of beautiful and started being my own."

— REMINGTON MILLER

What is it about loving ourselves that seems to be so

morally wrong and selfish? What is wrong with loving who I am in a world that only finds a way to hate me when I try to be myself? How many of you out there find it hard to love yourself because you see that self-love is often seen as a moral flaw? How do you see self-love? Is it immoral and selfish to love yourself? I know that growing up as a Christian; I was pushed to believe that vanity is a sin, and therefore loving myself was considered vain, which made me a sinner.

I remember feeling very miserable and ashamed when I would take a moment out of my day to try to love the person God had created me to be. I remember being told that to love myself was selfish, and that I should learn to put others first, for that is what a good person does. As I became older and hopefully a bit smarter, I questioned many of my beliefs that no longer served me.

As I questioned many of my thoughts and beliefs, I became very aware of how hurtful it was to keep this belief. **A belief that no longer serves you is a belief you have the freedom to let go of and replace it with a new one**. I found it rather messed up to think that loving ourselves is a selfish act. To some it may be a selfish act and a sin. But to me, it isn't. Maybe it was never clearly explained to me. Maybe it is okay to love yourself to a certain extent, or maybe it is vain and sinful.

No matter what it truly is in your eyes, this is what I know; this world needs more love, you need more love, and I need more love. We all need more love. And to love ourselves in, what some call, an unloving world, is not a sin to me. It is what will help us love and repair this broken world and the people who live in it. Loving yourself fully is the key that will unlock your most authentic self.

It is love that will help you get through the painful times and love that can transform any human experience from bad to beautiful. If the basic idea that loving one's self is vain and therefore a sin, then I find it understandable why so many of us think love is poison and love comes to an end. How could we not think that love is our enemy?

I know I did for the longest time. "Don't be selfish and share, don't be selfish and go help your brother clean up the house, don't be selfish and go help someone else do something they need to do." The only person who I really needed to help was me. Now, I am not saying that you should not be of service to others and take care of one another. On the contrary, I am saying that you need to love yourself, so that when the time does come to help another and be of service, you can come from a loving place and know that you have love and service to give.

Service is not supposed to be something you do out of obligation. Service is something that you should do voluntarily because your heart knows that caring for another is one of the greatest gifts that we can give to one another.

Many of us have a bad taste in our mouths that leads us to believe that loving ourselves, who God created us to be, is the selfish act of a sinner. No one wants to be a sinner, even though we are all created in sin.

This idea that leaves us feeling ashamed or even selfish when we love ourselves, is now embedded in our culture. I bring this to your attention to help you realize that loving and caring for yourself is not a selfish act or an act of sin.

Love is everything, and if you fully and truly love yourself, you will be led to serve this planet and all the wonderful people within it. This Earth is connected to each and every one of us. We need to bring the act of loving ourselves to the forefront of our being and embed it into our culture, that loving who you are and taking care of ourselves is just the wise thing for anyone to do. And if you want to live a life full of joy, excitement, and love, you will learn to embed loving yourself into your mind, heart and soul.

Become the light and love that you need, so that everyone else can follow your lead and see how beautiful life is. Become the one who let's go of this belief that loving yourself is a sin and a selfish act. Let go and replace it with a new and empowering belief that will not only support you but humanity as a whole. Let go and let love into your entire being and let it shine through you and into others as you walk by them. You have the ability to make this shift, and you deserve to make this shift, for you are in command of how you take care of you and love yourself.

3: YOU MUST LOVE YOURSELF BEFORE YOU CAN LOVE ANOTHER

Have you ever heard of the statement that says something like, "You can't truly ever love someone else if you don't fully love yourself first?" I am sure that many of you reading this today have heard this. It is something I used to live by for the longest time. For some reason it made sense to me until I realized that it no longer served me.

This belief stopped me from loving anyone or anything else. When I dove into this idea, I realized how much it affected my life in a negative way. As I really learned to live by this idea that I must learn to love myself before I learn to fully love another, what I discovered was life changing.

As I focused on this idea, I only found myself lonelier as time went on. You see, I couldn't ever fully let another person into my life, for I had built a fortress around my scared heart that wouldn't let others in. I knew that I still didn't love myself fully, so why let someone into my life and hurt them because I didn't fully love myself yet? It was such a challenge to let someone into my life and into my heart.

I had been through so many heartbreaks and damaging experiences that I never wanted to let another person in to break me and hurt me again. However, one day as I was talking to my father, he brought up something to me that changed my entire perspective. Something that changed my way of thought and ended up changing my heart.

Sitting across from me at the dinner table was my dad. My

dad and I were having some good conversations. We were talking about the past, the present, and the future. We talked about a lot which eventually led to him saying how he didn't know how to relate to me anymore, for he felt as though he was pushed out of my life and that I wasn't letting him be a part of it. These were some harsh words to swallow. Hearing my dad say he felt pushed away, and like he isn't a part of my life anymore, hurt. This truly broke my heart, which eventually led to a personal breakthrough.

My father means the world to me, and to have him say that to me, hurt me deeply, for I knew that it was my fault. The fortress that I had put up around my heart, not only blocked out others but also my family and those who loved me. That pain led to an almost immediate breakthrough for me.

I couldn't let it go on any further. My father is the type of person who belongs in everyone's life. He is kind, fun, funny, loving and such a joy! I have watched my dad be the strong, faithful, and loving foundation that both my brother and I needed in our lives. As he said that to me, I realized that the belief I had about not being able to love someone else until you learn to love yourself, was so inaccurate.

What I discovered was it's actually much easier to love somebody else than it is to love ourselves. You see, what stops us from building a loving relationship with ourselves, is that we know ourselves too deeply to fully love ourselves. Meaning we know our weaknesses, pains, and all the things that make us feel vulnerable, which is part of the reason why loving who we are is so hard.

While living in your body, you become very aware of what your weaknesses are, so you know where you fall short. With the knowledge of knowing where we fall short, what many of us do, is highlight those things in our minds, bodies and souls so much, that we live our lives focusing on and highlighting those weaknesses. And while many of us know our strengths, what we seem to do is downplay them rather than focus on them, like we do our weaknesses.

This, in turn, only destroys our relationship with ourselves and the love we have for who we are. As many of us downplay our strengths, we live a lower quality of life. We seem to live a life where joy doesn't stick around long enough to have an impact on our lives, all because we know we as individuals are imperfect. And knowing this, many of us live in that state of being imperfect. Too many of us know why we are imperfect, but few of us know why we are great.

Having a "why" to back up your imperfection will only strengthen that imperfection. Don't strengthen your imperfections with a "why." Highlight your strengths and give them a "why." In our bodies and our minds, we fall short of living in our greatness because we find it easier to highlight our weaknesses than our strengths. And because we have attached a strong "why" and a powerful emotion to them, it makes it that much easier to live in our weaknesses. So, because of knowing your weaknesses, you tend to pull away from all of that self-love and self-worth. And because you see your problems, flaws and pains and the greatness that is within each and every one of you, your self-worth is hidden behind all the pain and suffering.

These are just some of things that are causing many of you to be distracted and suppress your sense of self-love, self-worth, and self-value. With this knowledge, you should now feel a little bit more empowered, for you are now aware of a few big things that are causing you to suffer and live a life where darkness is king. With awareness on your side, you can begin to break free from your life-restraining chains and develop the self-love and self-worth that can empower you to live your best quality of life and build a powerful relationship with yourself.

Self-love is the key that will unlock your ultimate human potential and transform your human experience. By allowing yourself to accept love into your life, you can be on your way to living a successful life, where your relationships with yourself, others and God will complete you and always be there to pick you up when you are down. It will also help you find success in your career, in chasing your dream, and living a powerful and loving life that will become a life worth remembering.

11

THERE'S NO ONE LIKE YOU

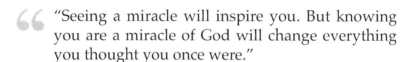 "Seeing a miracle will inspire you. But knowing you are a miracle of God will change everything you thought you once were."

— Tyler Joe Stratton

Another way in which you can build your powerful and loving relationship with yourself, is to understand just how important you are. There is a one in four hundred trillion chance of you being alive, yet you are here experiencing this amazing gift called life! Let that sink in for a moment and really understand just how wonderful and important you must truly be. I find it amazing to sit back underneath our wonderful night sky and realize that I am here and that you are here because we both matter.

Back in my hometown on summer nights, many of my friends would find themselves at the soccer fields lying underneath the amazing and beautiful night sky, reminiscing about our relationships, sports, the past, the future, and everything under the stars. There is something about looking up into the night sky that is lit up by all the stars painted by God, that brings out the philosopher in all of us.

You see, many of my friends and I would really dive deep into questions and topics about life as we spent our summer nights under the stars in those grassy soccer fields. However, this one night was a night which I will never forget.

As you know by now, my high school years were not the best, but this night was just one of the highlights to my senior year.

As we watched the Perseids meteor shower, we also fell upon a couple of questions. One of my good friends asked the question that struck us deeply: "Why are we here, and why were we given life?" As we sat there and pondered for a moment, I remember repeating a mantra that, as a little kid, had helped me get through my tough times growing up feeling so separated and alone.

I remember telling myself daily that, "You are here because this world needs you, and it needs everything you are and everything you are not." When repeating that old mantra that night, I realized at that moment, that the key to a loving and powerful relationship with yourself and the reason why we are here, is because we matter more than we can truly understand.

Understanding the truth that we are here because we matter, and that we should just learn to love our lives because we matter, helped me realize how many people really don't feel like they have any significant value. After discovering this truth, I started to dive deep into the question on how to love yourself more.

As I continued, I came to find so many different ways in which you can love yourself. However, the problem I discovered was that even though there are so many ways out there that you can love yourself, many still don't implement them or act on it. We may know we should love ourselves more. We may see that we had a better chance of winning the lottery ten times in a row than becoming a human being. We may know that love is everything, and if we want to enhance the life we live, then we must begin to love ourselves more. However, just because we know these truths, doesn't mean they are implemented and used correctly.

So why are we still having so many problems with our relationships? Why are there all these different ways and still no love on the streets we continue to walk daily? Why are so many people struggling with loving themselves? Why do people feel so unloved? Why are we afraid to feel loved by another?

Questions like these have been making me curious for such a long time, and as I explored these topics in search for the answer, what I found was that people make love complex with rules and regulations. That is why what I will be teaching you will be simple but powerful. There is no need to overcomplicate things. We have enough complications and learning to love ourselves no longer has to be one of them.

I will be giving you two very valuable and important discoveries that will help you identify your self-love and gain a deeper sense of self-love. By identifying and helping you to understand these two important values, you will live a life that is much more positive and loving. These two important points will empower you to live a better quality of life and experience a deeper love for yourself.

UNDERSTANDING YOUR INNATE VALUE

One of the most important values in which you must learn to familiarize yourself, is your innate value. This is your value as a human spirit. It is your deeper and more spiritual value. It is the value that you are endowed with by you just being alive.

Your innate value is such a great gift to understand because when you understand it, you realize that you are a miracle and a great gift from the highest God. You realize that you matter and so does your story and all your experiences while here on Earth. You realize that you are the ONE that was truly lucky because you are the ONE out of the four hundred trillion chances of being alive and with us today!

Did you know that you had a one in four hundred trillion chance of being a human and having a life on this planet? Well, guess what? You defied all odds. The reason you are here is because you matter. You were given life because you matter. **You have a purpose and a life that is worth living, and if you didn't, you wouldn't have been gifted this amazing opportunity. But you were**.

Think about it; a one in four hundred trillion chance. You are already winning. And you will continue to win as long as you remember and understand that you matter because you are here! It is that simple. You are here because you matter more than you may ever realize.

So, take some time to realize the miracle! This teaching alone has helped me get through some of my toughest times as a young teenager, who lived in the darkness and through the thoughts about ending it all. This lesson has helped me and many of the ones who I've shared this message and teaching with. I promise that if you can feel it and really understand that you are here because you matter, your life will begin to change at that very moment.

Become aware of the thoughts you think when it does change. Become aware of your heart when it begins to feel the loving light behind this truth. Become aware of the change that will happen to you when you dive into this important value. By identifying and highlighting your innate value, you and so many other people out there can have a life where they no longer feel subject to abuse and feel as though they are being ignored and just pushed aside as if they don't exist or matter.

You can start to enjoy your life even more once you understand and have identified your innate value. Once you understand your innate value, you will start to unlock your fullest life and begin to live it much happier, healthier, more positive and wealthier. A life worth living is a life worth remembering.

Right now, take a stand for yourself, your heart, and ultimately your life, and commit yourself to the understanding that your innate value is one of your greatest keys that will help you unlock a powerful and loving relationship with yourself. If you can truly understand that you matter, and that you are so very valuable, then I promise that you will realize what a game changer that is.

Your heart will begin to open up to living your fullest life. A life that is yours to live fully with an open heart that is unafraid of loving yourself or others. And if you learn this valuable life-changing lesson, you will become more open to loving yourself, and this world is in need of your special love.

Now is the time you begin the process of letting go of your past pains. It is time you begin to work on forgetting about what other people think of you and act like the miracle you really are. Realize this now before it is too late. Because every year we continue to age and hopefully get a bit wiser, even if we don't feel it, or see it.

You might be 45 and still unsure what you want to do with your life, or you might be 22 and think about how crappy your life is right now. However, no matter what age you are or what you are going through right now, you hold the power to change your life and your relationships today. All because you have the power of choice. If you want to experience a greater quality of life within, you must choose to walk that path and go after living that life every day.

The inner joy you feel or do not feel for yourself is dependent upon where you hold your attention. If you find yourself living a life or in a relationship where there is only cynicism, negativity, and distrust, you need to realize that it's a world of your own making. There is a miracle happening before your eyes every single day and that miracle is you.

There is a more beautiful world out there to be known, but you have to be able to see it within yourself first. You have to want to see it. You must be willing to take a leap of faith and step outside of what you know in order to live in a more extraordinary relationship with yourself.

EXPLICIT VALUE

Another life-changing discovery that will help you form a great relationship with yourself, is understanding and identifying your explicit value. Your explicit values are the things that you are good or great at. These are the things you enjoy, like writing, designing websites, reading, singing, being a mom, being a dad, being a good friend, working out or teaching others.

It is anything in which you are good at and continue to get better through your practice and dedication. Your explicit value usually is that one thing you have a natural tendency to turn to. It is that thing that you have a natural enthusiasm for.

All my life, my explicit values were athletics and teaching others how to get out of their pain and suffering. Sometimes discovering what your exact worth is can be challenging to uncover, and that is because they are the things that come so naturally to you that you overlook them.

The best way to get to know your explicit value is by getting to know yourself more, and by taking a few minutes every day to take a step back and reflect on your day and the life you have lived. Your goal is to find the common denominator or that reoccurring activity that you see yourself doing throughout your life.

Another perfect way to find your explicit value is to turn to those who love you and are close to you and ask them what they believe your top five strengths are. When I did this exercise, it opened my eyes and my heart! It made me feel so good about who I was and who I was becoming. It made me feel loved, confident, hardworking, and driven.

Ultimately, it helped me to uncover what my explicit values were and helped me to accept myself even more in-depth. When I did this exercise, I gave my best friend, my brother, and my father, a small piece of paper and had them write down what they believe my top five strengths were. However, before I handed over the piece of paper, I explained to them how important this was for me. I told them I needed help to see my worth and feel like I was good at something.

On the piece of paper, I wrote the following message: "I am doing this so I can become emotionally intelligent about myself. It will let me know what I need to reinforce in my life so I can be more confident, courageous, and joyful. I am doing this because this is what is going to help me see my explicit value."

I believe being vulnerable and explaining to them why I needed their help made them take this exercise more seriously and do a deeper dive before they wrote down just any strengths. I would advise you to do the same. Open up to those who love you. Explain to them how you need help, and I almost guarantee you that they will be there to offer you the support and clarity you need to see your exact value and just how amazing you indeed are.

Here is what my good friend, my brother, and my father said were my top five strengths. My good friend said, "you are a natural-born leader, a great speaker, a loving man, a great friend, and a person who sticks to his word." My father said, "you are a good-hearted man, hardworking, athletic, focused, and goal minded." And my brother wrote down the following list of strengths: "You have a great work ethic, you are driven, and goal-oriented." He also wrote down, "You have a huge heart and know how to care and love people. If you say you're going to do something, you do it—your words and actions match. You have great morals and values. You're a great listener, and you know how to understand and connect with people on an intense level. Oh, and you're the BEST brother in the entire WORLD!!! Love you always, Big Bro."

Those are the powerful words that I received from the

individuals who I asked. As I sit here on my couch, rereading and typing those words out, chills begin to overtake my body. A powerful energy of love flows quickly throughout my body as I type out those words and allow them to settle into my heart. The feeling you will get from doing this exercise will help you achieve the state of being you deserve to live in daily. A beautiful state of being where love becomes everything!

Once you identify the things you are good or great at, you must start to put your energy and focus into highlighting these things. For if we don't put our energy and focus into the things that we are good at, we will only devalue who we believe we are as an individual.

No more devaluing yourself! We need to build ourselves up so we can love who we are and start focusing on the more important things in life. We must learn to give ourselves a pat on the back and highlight what we are good or great at. For when we do this, we will start to feel more of that loving energy that exists in every one of us. Really "feeling it" is the key here. You must appreciate and value the things you are good or great at. And when you do, your belief in yourself will increase and your relationship you have with yourself will be one which you can become so proud of.

12

ACKNOWLEDGE ALL POSITIVE FEEDBACK

"Acknowledgement is the only way to keep love alive."

— BARRY LONG

ACKNOWLEDGE THE POSITIVE FEEDBACK FROM OTHERS

This one is a little bit easier to add to your daily life. However, it will take energy and focus, because it is something that many of us seem to lack. But no worries. We all have enough energy and focus for a bit of positive acknowledgement. From the time you wake up, to the time you fall asleep, a lot happens throughout the day. Learning to acknowledge the good things that happen throughout your day will only empower you to live a better quality of life while living with yourself.

For the next few weeks, I want you to do yourself a favor, and put a reminder into your phone that goes off three times a day. I set mine for when I wake up at 5:30 a.m., noon and 5 p.m., right before I get home. You can set yours to go off at whatever times are best for you. On these three reminders, write down a word that will help you look back on the hours that have gone by.

The word that is on my reminders is "reflect." What these words will do for you is remind you to reflect on the moments throughout your day that might have been overlooked but can bring some positivity and joy into your life.

For example: when it comes to getting feedback from others, you might hear them say, "Thank you for working so hard", or you might hear them say something more in-depth like, "You did a great job on (x)," or "You look beautiful today." The list is truly endless. However, the key that will unlock a greater sense of joy throughout your day is what you do during and after these moments are over.

That is why I am sharing with you a life-changing discovery that will help you feel the acknowledgment given to you. **The more acknowledgment that you allow yourself to feel, the more joy you will allow into your heart throughout your day**.

The next time you get positive feedback or any type of compliment, or even when something good happens to you in your life, start saying to yourself, "Wow, what a beautiful gift that was to receive that!" Say it and add a little smile. I use this all the time and it makes me feel so grateful, joyful and loved.

This exercise does truly help me feel happier about the life I am living. Most of the time, people don't acknowledge when they do something good for themselves, or when someone compliments them. Many of us just push it to the side because we haven't learned to value or love ourselves. We haven't learned to acknowledge ourselves or the compliments we get from others because we are carrying around this life-draining baggage that reminds us of our flaws. We all have flaws, but we also have beauty and greatness in us as well.

So, start embracing and taking in those moments and acknowledging them. When you learn to catch these moments as they happen and you say to yourself, "Wow! What a gift!", your life and the love you have for yourself will begin to change at that very moment!

ACKNOWLEDGE THE POSITIVE FEEDBACK FROM YOURSELF

This exercise will be tough; however, it will be a great one for you to do. I ask you not to overlook this one. You see, while in college, I learned this one while reading a life-changing book. And after reading this powerful book, I decided to write my own, which was so life changing, it really helped me develop more self-love and affection towards myself. And it will do the same for you. I promise.

Write yourself a letter of support. Think about this letter like the letter you might write to a friend you are concerned about. In this letter, list what you believe are your best and worst traits. This letter will include the steps you will be willing to take to help you feel better about yourself.

Don't be afraid to take some time on this letter. Do not rush through this letter, don't rush through this book, and more importantly don't rush through life! **No amount of rushing will bring you the success you seek. It is only the understanding and application of the lessons you have learned that will make the difference for you**.

Therefore, don't be in a hurry to finish this book, finish this letter or finish your life, because a complete reading of this book or quickly writing out your letter should not be your objective. Understanding and applying what you read and the lessons you write down in this book is the objective.

Do yourself a favor and turn on some music, open your heart and start writing a letter to yourself. Writing this letter helped me to reach a better state of mind and enjoy the relationship I have with myself. This letter is to be written to yourself out of love. Don't focus only on your best traits.

Learn to accept your worst traits and love yourself into acceptance of them, for you are you, and you can love all of you. After you write this letter, I have one more letter I encourage you to write.

While in college, I was put through an exercise that opened my eyes and changed my life that very day I did it. What I'm telling you might sound a little creepy, but I know from experience that it will help you see how valuable your life is right away. Your next letter that you should write is your own obituary.

Writing your own obituary is an exercise that is best approached with care, thoughtfulness and love. Your obituary will acknowledge the loss of your very special life. In your personal obituary, write down what you would like people to say about you when you are no longer here.

I want you to write down the significant events and attributes that you want people to remember you for. What impact will you leave on your friends, your family and the ones you love the most? What will your story be? What legacy will you leave behind? This obituary will help you recognize a few things.

One, being what you want your life to look like. Two, being what you are going to live for and three, how precious your life is. You are the one and only you. Recognizing that one day your time will come to an end, will help you see the beauty of your wonderful life here on Earth. Give it a shot and give yourself some time, if you feel up to it.

I know this will not be for everyone but try it with a caring mind and a loving heart. Get emotional. It is your life, and it should be emotional. This exercise will help to flush out the thoughts that are in the back of your mind and bring them to the front. It will help you see how valuable you truly are. This exercise has helped me live my fullest life. Now, the question is, will you let it help you live yours?

13

THE MORNING SHIFT

"You'll begin to live and love more fully the moment you have real reverence, deep gratitude and appreciation for life."

— Tyler Joe Stratton

Maybe you're not a morning person and you can't find the excitement toward the day; the only thing you feel when you wake up is the hate towards having to wake up and get out of bed. I know what it's like. I have been there. We all have been there.

Throughout my childhood, having to wake up at 4:30 a.m. to go to my babysitter's house was never fun! I always hated it when my father would come into my room, wake me up and take me out into the cold morning air to travel up to my aunt's house who used to babysit me.

I never enjoyed waking up for school, for college or for work. I never enjoyed anything about waking up until something within me shifted. I can't quite remember when this shift took place, but I do remember how I felt each morning after it took effect in my life. You see, I used to always hate waking up every morning. I hated everything about leaving my warm and cozy bed. That is until I gained a reverence toward life and realized that life is supposed to be fully lived with joy, love and excitement!

When I understood that life was supposed to be lived fully, I began to do whatever it took to figure out how to live a more fulfilled and impactful life. Waking up every morning and giving myself, and my life, the love it needs is my favorite way to begin my day!

I love to welcome each morning with a reverence toward life! Having reverence for your life will increase the quality of life you live! That is why the first decision you must make every morning is the decision to have reverence for your life every single day.

Having a reverence for your life every single day means you are aware of the fact that you are not guaranteed tomorrow, you are not guaranteed next week, you're not guaranteed three months from now or three years from now. It means you don't get to pursue the love you seek or the dreams you want to accomplish for the next ten, twenty or thirty years. Nothing in life is guaranteed. And if you deeply understand this, you will begin to see how precious your life truly is and experience it in a more joyful and loving way.

Make the decision to wake up every morning and remind yourself to have reverence for this life you have been gifted and to appreciate and be grateful for this breath. For this day, for this moment, and for the wonderful opportunities that await you every single day is going to seriously transform the quality of life you live.

It's a great way to begin to love yourself much more and your life as a whole. Having a reverence for your life will bring a sense of peace and gratitude your soul has been seeking for.

There is no better feeling than the feeling you experience when your soul is at peace and is joyful. That's why I enjoy welcoming each day with a smile and begin my mornings with a list of three things I am grateful for and three things that I can get excited about today. I simply love waking up. It's such a wonderful gift, and it's a gift that shouldn't be overlooked.

When you stop overlooking the gift of each day and your life, you will begin to show up every day and work toward becoming a better you. The more reverence you have for your life, the more you will realize that life is way too short. And the more you realize that life is short, the more you realize that you better begin to walk your own path. For we only have one shot at this life, and we should never allow the blessing of this day pass before us.

We have one life to live and I think a life worth living begins the moment you take this life just a bit more serious. Don't allow it to pass you by in a blink of an eye. Have some reverence for your life and show up being your best self. Wake up with excitement, enthusiasm and joy! You have the ability to wake up and generate the excitement, enthusiasm and joy!

All you have to do is become intentional and generate the thoughts that you need to think and begin to paint the picture in your mind that is going to excite you! Hold that picture in your mind and fuel it by feeding that positive picture more of your attention. The more you feed your mind positive and exciting thoughts, the more positive and full of life and energy you will begin to feel. You have a wonderful life that needs to be created and more importantly needs to be lived fully! Each day is a new opportunity toward living a life that you and others can deeply enjoy.

GRATITUDE

As I begin to have more and more reverence for my life, I found myself becoming much more grateful for who I am. I started to see just how special my life was and just how unique it was to be me. I found more of who I was, the more I pointed out the things I was grateful for. I found all the good that was buried deep within me that was hidden behind all the bad and ugly that I once focused so much on. But the best part of it all was I found a deeper friendship and acceptance toward myself.

Being grateful completely changed my life the moment I practiced it! And it can do the same for you and your life! However, the change will only begin to take place the more intentional you become with it. In other words, you must deeply feel the things you are grateful for. The benefits of practicing gratitude are nearly endless! People who regularly practice gratitude by taking a moment to notice and reflect upon the things that they are thankful for, tend to experience more positive emotions, feel more joyful, alive, sleep better, express more compassion and kindness, and even have stronger relationships.

The best things about being grateful is that you don't need to save it only for momentous occasions! I mean sure, you might feel rather blessed and grateful after receiving the job you always wanted or that new car, but you can also generate the feelings of being thankful for something as simple as your breath, a cup of coffee or your ability to hear the birds sing in the morning!

Research done by the world's leading scientific expert on gratitude, Robert Emmons, shows that simply keeping a gratitude journal regularly by writing brief reflections on moment for which we're thankful can significantly increase your well-being and overall life satisfaction.

The greatest way you can begin to truly experience the benefits of gratitude is by deeply describing the thing you are grateful for. Emerge yourself in the practice. Really feel that moment you were grateful for. Be in that moment fully, all over again, and once you are in that moment again begin to write it down. The reason for writing it down in your gratitude journal works is because it slowly changes the way you perceive your reality by adjusting what you are focusing on.

I love transforming the quality of life I live or the relationship I have with myself by writing down a few things I am deeply grateful for. The more specific you can get, the more you will be able to truly sense the deep change of bliss that will take place in your heart. So, don't just write down that "I'm grateful for my health." Get specific by writing, "I'm grateful for my heart that has never stopped beating my entire life. I am grateful for my lungs that allow me to breathe deeply and fully. I am grateful for every cell in my body that is helping me function and write this book." Do you see the difference?

I can feel the difference take place as I sit here comfortably on my couch typing this out. I am truly blessed and so are you! Point out the blessing and focus on the blessings, for that is what will help you and others get through the tough times and make life much more enjoyable!

Wake up and focus on your blessing. Wake up and realized how blessed you are. It's the little things that will help you gain the deeper joys in life you want to experience. The more you wake up feeling truly blessed, the greater your life and relationship with yourself will become! You see, on the days I would wake up and focus my mind on not wanting to be awake, I would find myself looking at life differently.

I wasn't excited and enthusiastic toward life, bettering myself, or wanting to help serve others the best that I could. When I would wake up not wanting to wake up and be annoyed at the fact that I had to wake up, my days would drag and oftentimes they would seem lifeless.

When my day felt lifeless, I felt lifeless. I felt much more negative because I saw much more negativity; I felt defeated because I didn't have the will or energy to prevail, and I felt much less confident in whatever it was that I was going to take on that day. **The way you wake up and show up each and every morning is a good indicator of what type of day**

you are going to have and what type of relationship you are going to build that day toward yourself.

The best way to continue to build a powerful and loving relationship with yourself is by giving thanks to God for the day and then set up some powerful morning habits that will help you practice self-care.

Self-care begins the moment you take full responsibility for yourself and your relationships. Know that you hold the power to step into the person who you know you truly are and begin to treat yourself the same way you would like others to treat you. It is just that simple.

If you would like others to treat you as the blessing you are, treat yourself and your life as a blessing it truly is each and every morning. Treat yourself with the same loving kindness you would treat a newborn child, the moment you wake up. Treat yourself with kindness, respect and self-care daily.

Know that this self-care isn't just a once-a-month type of thing. This self-care is a daily practice. Because taking care of yourself isn't always automatic, you must do one thing per day that will help you appreciate and love yourself more.

Your self-care could be taking a hot bath and relaxing to your favorite music in a candlelit bathroom. It could be taking ten to fifteen minutes to meditate. It could be reading a book, cuddling with your lover, or enjoying some Yoga. You name it; we are all different and know what will help us generate the most joy.

Your self-love affects your self-care and your self-care affects your self-love. So, start taking care of yourself by making a list of the seven different things you are going to do each week (one thing per day for seven days) throughout the week that will help you feel cared for.

Some things I have implemented into my life that have helped me to feel better about myself are: exercise three days per week, drink two big glasses of water when I wake up, which helps me bathe my insides and rehydrate myself from last night's sleep, meditate, read a good book every morning that will help me in some way and then just sit quietly with myself with no distractions and talk kind and meaningful words into my soul.

Self-care doesn't have to be complicated. Self-care is not tricky. It just takes a little bit of discipline, attention, and time. But with just a bit of care given to your self-care, the lack of self-love will begin to lift. You'll feel alive more and connected to yourself, the world, and the people around you.

You'll have gratitude in the small pleasures, and no problem will seem quite as challenging as it did before. You'll once again feel the charge you will need to deeply know that you are ready to take on the day and the challenges you will face. You'll once again be able to have the confidence, courage, love, joy, energy, and aliveness you need to be able to wake up and redesign a better quality of life and relationship with those who matter the most.

14

THE POWER OF FORGIVENESS

66 "Forgiveness liberates the soul. It removes fear.
That is why it is such a powerful weapon."

— NELSON MANDELA

The willingness to continuously forgive ourselves and others is the key that will help us unlock our aliveness in life, which will help us live a better quality of life and accept ourselves and others more peacefully. According to the Merriam-Webster Dictionary (2020), forgive means "to pardon," "to give up resentment," and "to grant relief from payoff." In other words, forgiveness is the need to accept that something happened entirely and cannot be undone. It is often a powerful gift that allows us to finish our unsettling business finally and feel free from the past, as well as feel complete and satisfied to continue.

Unfortunately, many of us don't give ourselves this gift because many of us would rather be right than to forgive. It is a sad truth, but the truth. We hold on to the painful memories and times that strip us away from experiencing true personal freedom and joy in our lives. We hold on to previous hurts, angers, heartbreaks, judgments, and find ourselves muddling through life with no excitement, comfort, or energy.

We're scared to be who we want to be because of the pain of those who were unkind to us. However, when we allow ourselves to let go of the previous hurts and be willing to forgive, we allow ourselves to experience personal freedom, peace of mind, vitality, aliveness for life, and the ability to live and love ourselves and others wholeheartedly. Life would be so much more peaceful if we could learn how imperfect all human beings are and allow mistakes to be made.

THE COSTLY CONSEQUENCE OF NOT FORGIVING

There is a costly consequence that each one of us pays when we are unwilling to be forgiving. When we are reluctant to forgive, we become blind to the results of blaming someone for their wrongdoing and holding long-term grudges against ourselves and others.

You see, the consequences that we pay consist of becoming much more exhausted, resigned and unable to connect with other people deeply. We lose vibrancy in our current relationships when we hold on to old events or people, or how disconnected we are from our vibrant and joyful life.

The price we pay for keeping all of our energies focused on the past will cause you to lack an enthusiastic life, develop poor health, have troubled relationships, experience loneliness, discouragement, and a feeling of isolation from one another.

Being unwilling to forgive someone is doing you more harm than good. Jack Canfield once said, "It can be hard to forgive and let go, but it's important to remember that harboring the resentment and holding a grudge can hurt you even more. The word "forgive" really means to give something up for yourself, not for them."

So why not do yourself a favor and give up the lack of vitality, poor mental, physical, spiritual, and emotional health you are dealing with and allow some room for a better quality of life. You must allow yourself to make room for healing to enter your heart truly. For you will never be able to fully recover until you first make space for love to come into your heart.

The real secret to being able to forgive and heal is to completely let go of the old painful thoughts and past pains so that new ideas and happier experiences can enter. For example, I have learned that there are many different laws of the universe. One being the law of gravity, which I am sure you all know, and another being called the vacuum law of prosperity.

The vacuum law of success states that you can't receive something until you are first willing to give that something away. Bear in mind, however, that "giving" means letting go of entirely or abandoning to another. For example, let's say that you need new clothing. You want a new wardrobe and a unique style that better supports how you want to feel and be seen. However, the problem you find yourself running into is that you don't have the money to buy the clothes you want, and you don't have any space in your closest because you have too many clothes as it is.

For you to receive what your heart truly desires, you must first make room for the desire to be accepted. So, if you want new clothes, you must first give away your clothes to make room for the new. Allowing yourself to let go of the people, thoughts, and past pains that have corrupted your overall well-being and vitality will be just as liberating as decluttering a cluttered space.

Begin to love yourself enough to create a safe environment in your heart that is conducive to the nourishment of your freedom! Let it go and be a prisoner of what has been holding you back no more! It is time to make some room for the good you so rightfully deserve!

THE HARDEST PART OF FORGIVING IS THE ABILITY TO FORGIVE OURSELVES

Forgiving yourself is as important as forgiving someone else. Time and time again, I hear people say that they overlook the person who hurt them or betrayed them, but they can't forgive themselves for what they have done. It comes as no surprise that we are most unforgiving when it comes to forgiving ourselves.

Many of us are very hard on ourselves, for we stay lost in the past, and we remember and blame ourselves time and time again for the old mistakes and disappointments we have lived through. With painful memories of our past mistakes and failures alive within us, we are quickly drained of our confidence and the aliveness of today. Whatever life has taken away from you, let it go!

When you surrender with an open heart (which is an inner knowing that God has your back and is there to take care of you at all times) and let go of the past, you allow yourself to be fully alive in this very moment. Letting go of your past mistakes and failures means you can truly enjoy the gift that the present moment has to offer you! If you stay locked up in the past, you will keep yourself in an unhappy state, which will result in living a low quality of life. Stop holding yourself in this state of being.

You deserve to feel free from the past and move on toward your bright future! To forgive yourself is the greatest of all the gifts you can give to yourself! For it is the highest and most potent form of active love, and in return for it, you will receive the peace, love, and joy you deserve to experience!

The best way to honestly let go of your past pains is to stop trying to let go and push away what it is you are trying to let go of. For example, let's say you are trying to let go of the damage your ex left you with. The sheer force of you trying to ignore the pain puts the spotlight on the pain. It really puts the focus on your pain, which then keeps your pain alive. Stop focusing on the pain when trying to let go of it. Build a new positive and hope-filled image in your mind to replace the image you hold that causes you to feel the pain.

You can do this by answering these couple of compelling questions. What is the opposite of everything you think, fear, and feel? What could replace everything you're trying to let go of? For example, let's say I am trying to let go of complaining all the time.

What I would do in order to let go of the complaining is to write down things I can replace complaining with. Instead of a list of things to complain about, I could create a list of things always to be grateful for. Once you paint your clear image of the opposite of what it is you are feeling, thinking, and fearing, begin to work on being that person daily.

Think about nothing but who it is you want to be and how you want to show up in the world, and soon you will become who you want to be. That is the proper way to let go of the negative past and replace it with the positive future you are now creating.

HOW TO FORGIVE THE RIGHT WAY

Now that you know why forgiveness is so essential, learning how to forgive the right way is necessary for your personal growth and freedom. Learning how to forgive ongoing is a beautiful daily habit to learn and get in to. To forgive the right way, we need to be sincerely willing to replace all the pain and all the suffering we are putting ourselves through with a positive image.

We must also begin to take control of what we can take control of. That means we must be willing to let go of the unfortunate mindset that no longer serves us. We must be willing to let go of our poor attitudes, opinions, and feelings that are not helping us to advance. We can all do this by reeducating and rewiring our minds. Instead of concentrating on the old thoughts, feelings, and emotions, you can begin to take control of the information that you digest, read, hear, and see. So instead of absorbing negative information, you can start to digest positive information that would better develop a more positive attitude, a more positive thought process, and belief system.

You can truly become the master of your thoughts and control what enters your mind. If you carefully choose what you want your brain to digest, you will eventually see a dramatic 180-degree turnaround. The more positive food you feed your mind, the more the positivity will overwhelm, overcrowd and ultimately push out the negative and unforgiving mindset you once had.

This will then be your newfound belief system that will begin to show itself in your actions and behaviors. That is why I put a filter on all my senses. I became very protective of what goes into my ears and my eyes. I paid more attention to who I listened to and who I took advice from as well as what I would read or watch. If it didn't help me heal and be a happier me, I wouldn't digest it.

The more I took control of the things I could control, the more positive and hopeful I felt. And to this very day, I am very strict about what I feed my mind with. When you begin to take ownership of your mind, the way you think and your attitude, you will start to move into the captain position of your future. As a result of becoming the captain of your future, all the negativity and turmoil in the world will not derail you from your life's purpose and, more importantly, your happiness.

However, taking ownership of the things you can control isn't the only way you can heal and forgive. Another way to heal and forgive is you must be willing to let go of your old life to create your new life. That's right. Your unique and happier you are going to cost you your old miserable you.

It's going to cost you your comfort zone and your sense of direction. It's going to cost you old relationships that no longer serve you. It's going to cost you not being liked by those who no longer want to grow with you and who don't want you to change. It's going to cost you who you used to be. But none of that matters at this point.

Those who you will lose during your journey are those who were not meant to be in your life. Once you let go of the old, the new will begin to replace the old. You will find those who you were meant to meet and who want to meet you on the other side. Then instead of being just liked by those who don't want to see you succeed and heal, you're going to be loved by those who want to see you succeed and truly understand the beauty of the new and improved you.

We all need to put a hold on being so caught up in our very own old, narrow perspective and start allowing ourselves to open up and have some new compassion toward ourselves and others. We may never like what has happened to us in the past, but we can learn how to accept what happened, learn from it and continue moving forward with hope, compassion, and love.

Taking a real and honest look at yourself will help you become more aware of incidents and qualities in yourself or within other people that we find rather difficult to accept and forgive. Most of the time, we like to gloss over and completely ignore how unforgiving and mean we can be towards ourselves and others.

To learn how to break through the lack of forgiveness, we need to take the first step to tell the truth about how we feel. This is step one. Be honest and truthful with yourself. For those of us who like to suppress our feelings and emotions to act friendly, to look good, or not hurt someone, opening up and being truthful and honest with yourself and your opinion might be a little bit uncomfortable at first.

I know it was hard for me to do at the very beginning. Lying to myself and wearing a mask that hid the truth seemed to be more comfortable than to face my feelings alone. However, what got me to overcome this uncomfortable feeling, was understanding how much freedom, peace, joy, love, and vitality was available on the other side of taking the many masks off and just being true to myself and toward others.

The following are some powerful exercises you can do today to help you open yourself up to forgiveness the right way.

BE HONEST AND TRUTHFUL

We should all stop and take a moment to get out a piece of paper and pen and start to make a list of all the important people with whom are in your inner circle (parents, girlfriend, boyfriend, boss, brother, sister, friends, etc.) including yourself at the very top of the list. Be sure to leave some space so that you can to write between each name.

After you have written down all the names, you need to stop at each name you come across and ask yourself, "Is there something I cannot seem to forgive in our relationship?" If there is not something to forgive, then take a moment to congratulate yourself and write down a list of things you are most grateful for when it comes to that specific person.

However, if there is something that needs to be forgiven, write them all down. Write everything that comes to mind, including; the event, feelings, thoughts, emotions, and everything else you can think of. Get very clear on the situation and relationship at hand. The clearer you become, the more personal freedom, love, peace, joy, and vitality you will begin to feel.

Once you get clear and begin to understand what you have not forgiven, you should then start to go over each specific item and ask yourself if you are ready and willing to accept the past as is and to forgive and let go of what was. If you find yourself very willing to let go, then congratulate yourself by explaining to yourself how grateful you are for this ability to let go so smoothly!

However, if you find yourself not as willing to let go of the specific items, find the courage to have a conversation with that particular person who you need to forgive and be ready to communicate clearly and respectfully what you have not been willing to forgive and let go of up to this very moment.

But before going into the conversation with that specific person, be sure to know what you want to say and communicate what you want to tell them clearly and respectfully. Communicate to them in a way that will reflect an inner self-love for yourself rather than a bad beat down toward the other person. Be there, in that conversation for yourself and the personal freedom, joy, and love that awaits you on the other side of that conversation.

If there is a reason why you can't talk to the other person or if you are just unwilling to talk to them but you still want to forgive them and experience your freedom once again, be willing to have an imaginary out loud talk with that person you need to forgive. I want you to speak your feelings out loud, as if the person who you want to and need to forgive is truly there.

This is a powerful tool that will help you complete any unfinished experiences. What I have noticed works well if that person is not there is either visualize them sitting across from you or use a friend who is willing to listen to you. Ask them to be there for you while you complete your process of forgiving that person who you need to forgive.

I find it more powerful if you do find someone to play the role of that person you need to forgive. But no matter what, the primary purpose of this exercise is to complete the words, "I forgive you, and I forgive me." This should be done in a deep and meaningful manner.

If these words don't ring internally valid for you, then you should keep pushing forward until they do. Once you experience the feeling of inner freedom, you then know that you have successfully forgiven yourself and that person. Don't stop until you find that personal freedom and let go!

Once we completely let go and detox our body, mind, and soul from all the past pains we have been holding onto, we need to make it our mission to be more aware of the moments we want to be unforgiving and make it our duty to not be cruel. The sooner we can let go of the problem, the sooner we will be living in a beautiful state of being. So today, let us make it our life's mission and work to live in a state of forgiveness for the rest of our lives.

I am confident that we will always react to people and circumstances when they arise; let us generate our inner willpower to quickly let go of these reactions and conditions that are holding us back from living our best quality of life. Learning to forgive ourselves and others quickly, frees up our lives and our relationships with The Big Three.

DEATH AND LIFE ARE IN THE POWER OF THE TONGUE

To create our best relationship with ourselves, we must stop speaking poorly of ourselves. There have been multiple times in my life where I have belittled myself, complained about myself, struck hate toward myself, and made myself believe that I was never good enough or smart enough.

A powerful and loving relationship will never be built if you speak poorly of yourself. Never give yourself a conscious moment to forgive yourself for the thoughts you think and the things you say. It wasn't until I learned that death and life are in the power of the tongue, that I truly began to realize how self-sabotage through self-talk no longer served me and my higher purpose.

Although the negative self-talk and self-doubt still lives within me, it no longer controls my reality as much as it once did. It wasn't until I implemented a powerful technique into my life that I could begin to overcome the self-sabotage and self-talk so I could continue to build a powerful and loving relationship with myself.

I suggest you do the following. For the following technique has helped me tremendously while writing this book and so many other times, and I know it will help you too!

When we begin to hear that little voice inside our heads that strikes hate, doubt, fear, lack of love, confidence, and belief into our lives, we must begin to forgive ourselves right then and there. For every wrong thought we hear, we need to generate a good one.

Begin the process by speaking powerful affirmations to ourselves like "I forgive myself for speaking badly about myself." "I am confident in my ability to be loved and give love." "I am enough." I know this seems like it will not work, but you talking to yourself, calling yourself stupid and ugly, definitely makes you feel poorly about yourself, doesn't it? Doesn't all the self-sabotaging talk you speak unto yourself cause you pain, suffering, and negativity? I am sure it does! So why not do the opposite for yourself and speak some forgiveness into your life? Remember, what you say is what you get.

Speaking about life and forgiveness daily will help you achieve a better quality of life. Although this is a simple but powerful technique, you can't afford to overlook it and not speak it. If death and life are truly in the power of the tongue, then why not control what you say? Why not speak about bringing love, light, hope and forgiveness into your life?

I truly believe that you can change your world by changing your words; for every conscious thought that makes you doubt yourself, you must get good at generating a positive thought and speaking positive words that will remind you that you are enough and that there is hope, and you are the hope.

I believe in you all. We are all good enough, and we all

have the power to generate a more hope-filled and forgiving life.

Aside from forgiving ourselves, we must be willing to forgive ourselves forever in an ongoing manner. That means that at any time in the future when we find ourselves in a similar negative thought, we cannot indulge in it and allow it to harm our day.

Instead, we must remember that we already forgave ourselves once and have made a commitment to continue to forgive ourselves forever. This can be a difficult discipline to adopt, but it must be learned! Learning how to choose the ability to forgive ourselves in an ongoing manner so we can continue to develop compassion and love for ourselves, is what will help save you from your dark days.

If we find we cannot forgive ourselves right now, then we need to use our voice and get very clear on what we need to forgive to move beyond the pain point, and not take the negative feeling everywhere else we may go. If you are feeling stuck and feeling unwilling to forgive yourself, you need to begin the healing process by asking yourself, "How long do I need to pay for this specific misdeed or mistake?" or "How long must I continue to suffer?" or "If I can't forgive myself right now, then what needs to happen to forgive myself?"

Getting clear on what steps and actions you need to take to completely forgive yourself is an essential step to follow. The best way to answer the questions above is to understand that if you have something in your mind that is hurtful and you want to forgive yourself for it, what you need to ask yourself is, "How long do I need to hold on to this for?" I say as long as you'd like a little child to keep it. Don't hold on to anything for too long. Forgive, let go, and, more importantly, move on with a hope-filled mind and heart.

Everyone needs to forgive themselves for something, so everyone who reads this book needs to create a step-by-step plan to come to terms with so that they can begin to forgive themselves. We can be very hard on ourselves. Thus, once you are willing to forgive yourself, you must take massive action by setting up a plan and a time limit to do so. Don't leave it up to chance. Gain clarity and start working towards ways to stick to your word and to forgive yourselves for the past pains.

You have suffered long enough, my friend. Stop yourself from wasting any more time in the past. You only have one life to live and spending your life living in your past is no way to live.

You need to be quick to forgive yourself, others, and God before you find yourself withering away, unable to feel vibrant, confident, and joyful. The price you pay is too high to be unwilling to forgive yourself, others, and God. You have one life. Remember that.

MASTERING FORGIVENESS

Our freedom would rise exponentially if we lived in a continuous state of forgiveness with ourselves, others, and God. Likely, we will always make mistakes, and because of this truth, it would be helpful if we could learn to quickly forgive and let go. Your relationships toward The Big Three would be more connected and more powerful if you were always willing to forgive. That is why mastering forgiveness is essential. You can build the life and relationships you want if you begin to work on mastering forgiveness.

Mastering forgiveness takes a lot of time, energy, and effort. But I promise you it is worth it all. To be able to forgive everyone who comes to mind, and to forgive yourself for every mistake, upset, flaw, problem, guilty feeling or negative thought will take a lot of work but know that you deserve to experience the personal freedom that is waiting for you once you let go and open yourself up to forgiveness.

You all can do this. You just must be willing. As soon as you are ready, life will begin to work its magic and begin to heal your heart, mind, body, and soul. So be sure to remind yourself often to forgive yourself and those who need your forgiveness.

You can do this by practicing the Ho'oponopono, which is a Hawaiian practice of reconciliation and forgiveness. Practice the Ho'oponopono by saying the following words of forgiveness aloud and with feeling over and over again:

Ho'oponopono
    "I am sorry."
    "I love you."
    "Please forgive me."
    "Thank you."

Remember, forgiveness is the most powerful tool we have for transforming ourselves, our lives, and this world. The personal freedom and zest for living are available for each of us: Let us forgive ourselves, others, and God for anything and everything, for therein lies the promise of an abundant and genuinely joyful life.

15

CREATING POWERFUL INTENTIONS

> "We shouldn't hope to end up one day a magnificent, strong, beautiful, capable, kind, loving, person. We should start living like that today, so we become that. Who we become is not an accident, but a purposeful intent."
>
> — BRENDON BURCHARD

The power of intention setting is a critical factor that plays in all areas of our lives. By simply intending to create powerful and loving relationships in your life, you will begin to nurture that result and then receive the thing you have been nurturing.

A tree cannot become itself without mother nature first nurturing it. While going after my dreams and ambitions, I have discovered that it is the intention that is the starting point of every thought and purpose we will go after. I have become aware of the creative power that intention truly is and how it helps to fulfill all of our needs, whether that be for loving relationships, love, money, or influence.

Everything that happens in the universe or our lives begins with the intention that we set. When you decide to become more loving, go to the gym, or call up family members, it all starts with the plan to do so. No matter what your next move will be, it will always come after the intention you set forth.

The sages of India observed thousands of years ago that our deepest intentions and desires ultimately shape our destiny. "The classic Vedic texts known as the Upanishads declares, You are what your deepest desire is. As your desire is, so is your intention. As your intention is, so is your will. As your will is, so is your deed. As your deed is, so is your destiny." (Chopra, 2005).

You do genuinely become whatever your intention is set on. That is why it is vital to know what an intention is and how you can harness the power of intention to create anything your heart truly desires. **Who you want to become is possible, but first, you must set the intention to be it**.

One of my favorite New York Times Best-Selling authors, Deepak Chopra, explains intention as "a directed impulse of consciousness that contains the seed form of that which you aim to create and become. Like real seeds, intentions can't grow if you hold them. Only when you release your intentions into the fertile depths of your consciousness can they grow and flourish." To become the person you have always wanted to become and have the relationships your heart truly desires, you must plant the seed into the fertile soil of your mind.

You can become the person you were always meant to become right now by setting the intention to be just that today. Because at the end of your life, while you are lying there on your deathbed, the things you are going to look back on are not going to be all the success and achievements you have made for yourself. For that's just a lonely world.

Instead, you are going to look back as a delighted individual who is going to feel fulfilled, joyful, loved, and peaceful because of the relationships you've developed, the friendships you have made, the love you allowed in, and the legacy you have created.

The riches you will want to experience at the end of your life can be found in the relationships you intentionally create along the way. Let us begin setting our intention today so you can have the relationship you have always wanted with The Big Three.

Here are the five steps that will help you capture the creative power of a plan to create the life, relationships, and results that your heart truly desires.

STEP 1: PLANT YOUR SEEDS OF INTENTION

Before I jump into this one, be sure to stop what you are doing and go onto any podcast application and subscribe to my podcast called The Ultimate Human Connect Podcast. In this podcast, it is my mission to significantly improve the quality of life you live by teaching you how to feed, nourish, master and maintain a healthy mindset, heart, health, and soul so that you can begin to experience a life that you have always deserved to live.

This podcast will help you rule your inner world so that you can begin to live a better outer world. It's a podcast focused on upgrading your inner world like your thoughts, behaviors, emotions, perspective, beliefs, and so much more so that you can improve your outer world.

If you are trying to become a better version of yourself so that you can begin to love the person you are, this will be a great podcast to check out!

Most of the time, it is our inner world that rules our life. Getting stuck up in our thoughts, emotions, and memories can make it rather difficult to turn down the internal dialogue and create a peaceful state of mind. However, there is a place beyond the chatter where the state of pure awareness rests that is sometimes referred to as the gap.

The gap is the most elusive space for human beings to enter. For it is a place of solitude. It is a quiet and peaceful place that exists behind your thoughts, beliefs and emotions. In other words, it's a clean and quiet place that is within your mind where you can begin to plant positive seeds of intention to begin to craft a better version of yourself.

The best way to experience this space called the gap is through meditation. Over time meditation can help take you beyond the chatter of your mind and into the silence and stillness of consciousness where your blank canvas waits for your arrival.

For I believe that when you enter this state of being, you have the opportunity and freedom to paint the picture that you want to see and become. This is the state you want to be in so that you can begin to plant your seeds of intention and desire into your mind and become the person you always knew you could be.

STEP 2: EFFORTLESSLY LET GO AND RELEASE

Once you have found your peace of mind, it is now time to effortlessly let go and release your intentions and desires you have thought of in this meditative state of being. After your meditation, you will find yourself in this peaceful meditative state of being where you feel grounded, centered, supported, and love.

It is in this quiet place where all the impossible become possible. When you feel grounded, focused, supported, and loved, you know God is working in your favor. After you set an intention and see yourself being the best person you know you are, let it go and release it. In other words, effortlessly stop thinking about it and trust that the universe and God has your back and your seed will soon begin to flourish.

STEP 3: FOCUS ON THE POSITIVE

Your intention becomes much more reliable and more potent when you focus on the positive and come from a place of contentment rather than focusing on the negative and feeling the sense of lack or need. You want to always come from a place of abundance and positivity if you can. If you are not feeling so positive and abundant, be sure to practice abundance meditations.

Bob Proctor has a perfect meditation I turn to a lot when I am not feeling positive and abundant. It is currently called the Abundance Meditation. This meditation will help you come from the place you will want to go from to manifest the intentions and desires you have set forth. I'll be sharing this meditation through my YouTube channel, so be sure to check it out. Just search for Tyler Joe Stratton, and you will find me and the meditation. Once you land on my page, go to playlists and click the table that says The Big Three– Meditation Practice. There you will find the meditation that I use almost daily.

Feeling abundant, centered, and positive will help you overcome other people's thoughts, opinions, and doubts, which is something you will need to do along the way toward becoming your best self. Your best self knows that no matter what you go through, everything will be alright. Set your intentions, focus on staying positive, and live congruently to who you know you can be.

STEP 4: EVERYTHING IN LIFE IS TEMPORARY

Everything in life is temporary. The key is not to get attached but instead, learn to flow with the natural current of life. Let go of your firm attachments to any specific result and live with the wisdom and understanding that everything in life is temporary.

Being attached to anyone or anything is based on fear and insecurity. Like I wrote in step three, focus on the positive. Feeling fearful and insecure will not get you to the place you want to be or feel or allow you to be successful in your life and relationships.

Detach yourself from the outcomes and events that life will toss at you. For when you can detach yourself from life's outcomes and events, you will feel much more powerful and positive. When you truly separate yourself from the result, what you are doing is building your faith in God. Because in the back of your mind, you know that God has your back, and that everything is going to work out as it should. Build the faith, let go and allow new opportunities and openings to come your way.

STEP 5: LET GOD HANDLE THE REST

Your desired and well-thought-of intentions have set the powerful universe in full motion. Have faith that God and the infinite organizing intelligence will peacefully fulfill all your heart's highest purposes and desires. Stop yourself from listening to that voice inside your head that says if you want to be successful, you have to be in charge; that obsessive action and hard work is the only way you are ever going to achieve the life and relationships you want to have.

Don't try to force your way toward your intentions, desires, and success. For it may not be as good for you as the one that is coming naturally. I know this from experience. I fought many uphill battles to end up nowhere near where I wanted to be. But the moment I let go and let God handle the rest, the path showed itself more clearly and effortlessly.

When it showed itself, I knew that writing this book would be the first step toward the life I wanted to live. But If I kept battling uphill and being a control freak, I would have never heard God speak confidence, courage, and joy into my heart. I would have never written this book or started my podcast or be the better man I am today.

Do yourself the same favor I gave myself, let go and release your intentions into the fertile ground of pure potentiality and allow the seeds of intention to bloom when the season is right.

PART II

KEY #2: BUILDING A RELATIONSHIP WITH OTHERS

"The most important single ingredient in the formula of success is knowing how to get along with people."

— THEODORE ROOSEVELT

One of the most profound experiences you can have in your life is a powerful and deep connection with other human beings. There is something about a powerful and deep connection that can light your soul on fire.

The second key that will help you live your fullest life and love your life more, is learning how to build powerful and loving relationships with others. Powerful and loving relationships with others will help you feel happier, healthier, more positive, and give you more love in your life. Without them, life can feel kind of… dead.

This dead feeling that I am talking about usually comes into play during certain times throughout our long relationships with our significant others. I have met so many people who jump into a new relationship with the utmost excitement at having found their new significant other. Their relationship is great for a while, but what seems to happen over a period of time, is that the relationship starts to die and wither away like a plant that never gets enough care.

As time goes on and our relationship's flame begins to dwindle down, we find our relationship with that other person loses its strong connection. Losing that strong connection can be painful and scary, but by understanding this one thing, you might be able to rekindle the flame and rebuild that strong connection with them once again.

You see one of the main reasons we no longer feel as close or connected to that one person who comes to mind is because we get so caught up in the routines and habits, to the point the relationship becomes monotonous. We lose spontaneity and that deep meaningful connection because we know what to expect after getting to know that person on a deeper level. And all of the sudden what happens? We stop seeing the beauty we once saw in the beginning. We stop feeling the magic in the very person who we had met in the beginning and fell in love with. We lose our purpose to grow and to make a relationship a powerful and loving one.

Over time, people stop connecting with their purpose, which is also known as the reason why they are in a relationship in the first place. They stop putting in effort over a while, and then the relationship starts to die. I have also seen many people experience this dead feeling when they go through a tough break up, divorce, or a near-death experience. I know many times throughout my life, I have let this dead feeling creep into my life because of the relationships I was or wasn't in.

I used to let the relationships I was or wasn't in define the quality of life that I was living. Growing up in a broken home, there were plenty of times when I let my parents' anger and hatred for each other, define my relationship I had with them as well as with myself. I was the kid who always reacted in a very angry way when I would see my parents or the people I had to have a relationship with in conflict with one another.

Anytime I saw conflict, I would enter a very aggressive state of being where I would do or say anything to make the conflict stop. Hate ran deep in my heart when I saw conflict between others, and I would let it ruin the quality of life I was living when around it.

Conflict destroyed my heart and my life and that is why anytime I was around conflict, I would say cruel and foul things and even get abusive towards others and myself. I used to let conflict destroy my mind, my body, and my spirit. Conflict struck me in ways that made me believe my life was being threatened.

For many years, I remember always believing that when conflict was around me, people were just trying to destroy my heart. I remember thinking that they were destroying the one thing that makes me who I am today, my heart. If you destroy my heart, you are taking my life. And if you are trying to destroy my life, I will do everything I can to fight for it and destroy yours.

That was the battle I was in for many years when I had a poor relationship with myself and with others. However, what I learned over the years has truly saved my life and relationships with others, and it can do the same for your life. I just wish someone would have told me what I am about to tell you sooner so I wouldn't have suffered so much. But we cannot learn without pain.

As children, we all need someone to take care of us in order to survive. However, as young teens and adults, that doesn't mean that you have to let the people you are in a relationship with, ruin the quality of your life. You are in complete control of how you will let a situation or relationship define you, and the quality of life which you are living.

You don't have to be upset just because the person you are in a relationship with is upset. They are their own unique person, and you are yours. There are two individuals in one relationship together. The two of you do not make one. You can come together as one but know that there are two of you and you can only ever be in control of your one mind, thoughts, emotions, and environment. Not yours and your partners.

Take care of yourself and make sure you are grounded to your values and living intentionally and congruently with the person who you want to be. **For when you are trying to live the best version of yourself, you will notice that the relationships you have with others will not be as harsh, and won't affect your life in a negative way, even when they are being negative and conflict strikes in their life**.

Many people happen to take their problems and just pass them off so freely to others. This isn't a bad thing when you know how to handle their issues and conflicts and know how to show up during those times. However, when you start to notice you are carrying around other people's luggage, remember to show up as your best self. For when you show up as your best self, you will be ready to deal with that person's tough day or negative news and help them through it. But you do not have to make their issue your issue unless you decide you want to.

This is a lesson which I didn't grow up learning. I believed that the relationships I had with my parents and others defined who I was, and I let them create my quality of life by allowing the quality of their day dictate the quality of my day. The quality of your life will increase once you learn how to build powerful and loving relationships with others. You will experience more joy, passion, ecstasy, excitement, love, and meaning once you begin to develop powerful and passionate connections with others.

Your relationships are indeed the basis for all of life's most significant rewards and toughest struggles. If you want to increase the quality of life you are living, you have to open your heart up once more and allow healthy relationships back into your life.

When I dove deep into the different ways in which I could build powerful and loving relationships with others, and how relationships could improve my life, and started taking what I had learned and incorporating into my life, I began to watch my life change. I no longer let relationships define the quality of life I lived. Your relationship you have with others will no longer affect you unless you let it. But you must first understand why the relationships we have with other people are worth building in the first place.

.

16

WHY BUILD A RELATIONSHIP WITH OTHERS

"Getting closer to the people who make you feel less far away will result in a life well lived."

— Tyler Joe Stratton

Throughout my life, I have found it rather easy to fall under the pressure of wanting to fit in to a certain group. I always wanted to fit in and be accepted rather than to stand out and be bullied or alone. However, as time went on and I began to heal myself and learn to accept me for me, I learned to step away from those people who made me feel like I had to change myself in order to fit in.

As I began to slowly step away from certain groups that didn't accept me for me, what I learned was that if those people don't have the same likes and values as I did, what they brought to my life wasn't of importance. Once I realized this, I found myself saying to myself, "Don't stay with people who make you feel far away, unimportant, or not valued. They are not bad people; they are just not your people. You will find your people and once you do, you will begin to see the beauty that relationships have to offer."

A powerful and loving relationship is a beautiful gift that can give you certainty, meaning, a sense of aliveness and a powerful source of confidence, courage and joy. What's the secret to enjoying the relationship of your dreams? How do you spark passion and love, even in moments of conflict? Your relationship should be your greatest source of pleasure. If you're struggling with your partner or would like to take your relationship to the next level, then read on!

As the naturally social creatures we are, we all crave powerful and deep relationships with others. Relationships are what we remember at the end of our lives. Not the material wealth and empire we've gained throughout the years.

At the end of our lives, we will want those who have loved us around us. Not the cars, clothes and diamonds. If you know this to be true for you, like it is for me, then let us take a committed vow together and start making it our intention to create powerful and loving relationships in our lives so we can start to live a life worth remembering.

As humans, the relationships we create with other people are so vitally important to our mental, emotional, and spiritual well-being, and really, to our overall survival as a species and our family line.

Deep inside all of us, there are many common grounds that we can find hidden behind every loving man or woman, every evil and dark bully, and every human being. We all want to feel connected and loved. Which is why we all must learn how to build powerful and loving relationships. If it was everyone's goal to create powerful and loving relationships with other people, our world would be a more peaceful and loving place.

CAST AWAY

While in the movie Cast Away, directed by Robert Zemeckis and starring Tom Hanks, Helen Hunt and Paul Sanchez, Tom Hanks, also known as Chuck Noland, is a man who becomes stranded on a deserted island. At one point in the movie, Chuck starts talking to a volleyball, which may not be the healthiest behavior for someone to do. However, it was his compulsion to find someone or something to accompany him in order for him to feel connected and safe.

His relationship to this volleyball might be the reason why he stayed alive. It was his compulsion to connect and have a relationship with something, even a volleyball.

No matter the type of healthy relationship you have, whether that be a romantic relationship with someone you love, a strong friendship, or familial relationships, the truth is, they all count and are all very important to our mental and emotional well-being.

These relationships you have with others can really help make your life feel full of life and it can help make for a healthier life. But what does a healthy relationship look like? I know, coming from my own broken home, I didn't always have someone to look up to, to see what a healthy relationship looks like even when the going gets tough. So that's why I made it my life's mission to dive deep into my studies, to learn what it takes to create powerful and loving relationships with others. Because truth be told, relationships will always be in your life and can be the best part of your life if you create them to be. You cannot escape them either.

Knowing and deeply understanding this truth, really got me excited to discover what a positive relationship looks like when shared between any two people who are in love; who support, encourage, and help one another become their best selves.

After diving deep into my studies and talking to many different families and friends who have been in long-term relationships as well as terrible break ups, what I have found are some common grounds which they all spoke about. In order for people to have a healthy relationship, they tend to create a vision for what they really want in their relationships; actively listen to one another, communicate openly and fully without feeling judged about what they are saying to the other, trust and respect each other, never take anything they say out of anger to heart (for it was never about you), and find time to connect with each other without distractions, just to name a few.

Furthermore, I would like to state that while you don't have to be romantically involved to enjoy the amazing benefits of a healthy relationship, there are many studies that have been conducted on the positive effects a healthy relationship can have on your overall health. Here are a few more reasons why you should get yourself involved in a healthy relationship with others:

RELATIONSHIPS WILL HELP YOU TO STRESS LESS AND BECOME MORE

Whether they're friends, family members, intimate partners, mentors, colleagues or people you're just getting to know, working on your relationships can be great for your mental health. Being able to deeply connect to just one person can significantly improve the quality of life you live and help you get closer to other people in your life.

In this day and age, it might come as a complete surprise to you that being in a committed relationship is linked to less production of cortisol levels within your body. When your body is stressed, it releases adrenaline and cortisol. Adrenaline can raise your heart rate and blood pressure, which in turn can damage your overall health.

This does, in fact, suggest that those who are in a healthier relationship with another person, are less likely to experience psychological stress. Which might be another surprise, considering many of us out there have this belief that relationships are the root of all evil and all they cause is one to feel broken hearted, miserable and stressed.

However, when in a powerful and loving relationship with others, there are amazing benefits, such as the social and emotional support that comes with having a partner by your side, which can be a great tool in fighting against stress and hard times. I know this has come in handy for me many times when I've found myself out of my comfort zone.

I love being able to fall back on my partner or my business team, to help me face the feeling of being out of my comfort zone.

Being a part of a very powerful business team has helped me become more comfortable with being uncomfortable. I know that every time I felt out of my comfort zone and didn't want to do the thing that would make me feel uncomfortable, I had an incredible team to rely on to help me push through the stress, overwhelm or the feeling of being uncomfortable.

I love having such a powerful group of positive people who I am in a close relationship with help me get through the uncomfortable, difficult and uncertain moments in my life. The relationship I have built in my business has really helped me to step into a more confident and less stressed me. Through these relationships I have built, I have learned the great truth that we are so much better together and together we can begin to accomplish our dreams so much faster.

If you are looking to join a powerful group of positive, uplifting, supportive group of people with me as well as learn how to make an income that is not tied to your time, be sure to reach out to me via email at tylerjoestratton@gmail.com. I'd be more than happy to assist you in doing the same things that I have had the privilege to do with such wonderful and caring people.

RELATIONSHIPS WILL HELP YOU TO HEAL BETTER

There is also evidence suggesting that couples who live together are happier than those that live alone. I know that sounds a bit crazy, but it is true. Remember, we were born to connect and build relationships with one another, not hide away and live alone.

According to an article written by Huffington Post called "Marriage and Health: Study Suggests Marriage Can Help with Recovery After Heart Surgery," researchers at Rutgers and Emory universities concluded that married people who have had heart surgery are three times more likely to survive. The researchers followed five hundred people (who were married and single) who were undergoing coronary bypass surgery.

The lead researcher, Ellen Idler, stated "When asked whether they would be able to manage the pain and discomfort, or their worries about the surgery, those who had spouses were more likely to say yes." There have been many studies that have been shown that married people are less likely to get illnesses.

A study conducted in Stockholm (Hope, 2009) found that those who are married or in a relationship during their middle ages are about fifty percent less likely to develop Dementia than those who are single.

Health to me is one thing that I make sure I take care of daily. For I know without my health, my dreams are not possible. I know that my health must come first if I want to be a man who is remembered for helping others live a better quality of life.

That is why the first thing we all must take care of is our health, whether that be our mental health, physical health, spiritual health or health within the relationships we have with others and God. We must find a way to stay healthy, and partners can be the way to help us find our optimal health.

Staying healthy and happy for myself, goes a lot further

and means so much more when I make it my purpose to stay healthy for my mom, my dad, my brother and God. For I know that when I lack the health, I become miserable and unhappy. And that is not how I want to show up in my relationships.

They deserve the best of me, and I know that my health will help me give them the best of me. What I am really trying to say, is that whether it's having someone there to help remind you to wake up to take your medication, having someone there to motivate you to develop your dream, or have someone there to help take your mind off the pain and stress you are struggling with, relationships with others can help you gain better healing and health by supplying you with the love, support, and confidence that you might need.

Sometimes they know you more than you, and that can really help you when you are being stubborn and ignore the truth that your health is depleting. Healthy relationships can also lead to healthy behaviors. I love this truth. I know that while living with my brother throughout my life, we really set each other up to succeed in many different areas of life, one of these being the way we helped each other by challenging one another to achieve a better overall healthy lifestyle.

Not ever wanting to lose one another or be without one another too soon, it has helped us build a powerful, loving and fun relationship throughout our years of brotherhood. Being in a relationship can create healthier behaviors because you will always have someone there to challenge you to reach for your best like my brother has for me throughout my entire life.

I know the relationship I had with my brother helped us both to eat healthier, try different fasting practices, try to drink a gallon of water per day, try new and different supplements, run in the Spartan Races, and always help each other live our healthiest lives so we can be there for one another for as long as God allows us to.

Having healthy relationships can really set the perfect tone for an upgrade to your overall quality of life. There is something about loving someone that makes you want to be as healthy as possible. A healthy you is a happy you, and a happy you can support, love and cherish the time you have with those who really care about you. It is a lot easier to live a happy, healthier, more positive and wealthier lifestyle when you surround yourself with people who are doing the same and are keeping you accountable.

RELATIONSHIPS WILL HELP YOU GAIN A GREATER SENSE OF PURPOSE

It's a natural need for humans to want to feel needed, and to know that they are a part of something bigger than themselves. Something I have noticed throughout my life is that so many people are trying to find purpose in their life. They strive to feel like they are doing something good for themselves and for others.

When thinking of their purpose, many people try to do something in their life to help improve themselves, others, or the world in some way, shape, or form. Many people try to take on the world and try to figure out a way to make it better just to find their purpose. This is great and all, but if you are someone who is struggling to discover your goal, look no further than at the relationships you have with yourself, others, and God. For it is the relationships you have with The Big Three that will bring you a greater sense of purpose in your life.

By giving your best self to The Big Three, you will be able to leave this world with no regret and feel like your life meant something. You will deeply know that you were loved. The relationships you have in your life will give you a more profound sense of meaning and purpose.

Having a higher purpose in your life can increase the quality and perhaps the number of years you live, and who doesn't want to experience both of those? Increased vitality and years sound like a great life to me! More time and more joy! That's what I am after. But just because I want more time to live doesn't mean I am afraid to die. For I am not afraid of death. I am afraid of not living while I am alive. I am afraid of not living a long and full life, full of loving and powerful relationships that bring a deeper meaning into my life, and relationships that will help me unlock my fullest potential.

I am scared to waste my life away and not live out my purpose. To live my purpose is my mission, for I know that you and I both were designed by God to do something or to be a part of something meaningful and purposeful.

Making it our purpose to develop powerful and loving relationships can do a lot for you, for me, and, more importantly, for our planet. If we develop a purpose-filled connection within ourselves and begin to cultivate real inner peace and joy within our hearts, we will only have that to give to others, and that will be a gift to God.

That is why I believe that it only makes sense that the better our relationships are with The Big Three, the happier and more alive we will become as individuals, and the better we can begin to make the world. For more joy we feel and have in our daily lives, the more our quality of life will increase. And when the quality of our life increases and celebration begins to take over our hearts, those are the moments which we will remember the most.

Don't waste your life away by waiting for these moments to happen to you. Live your life with a purposeful mission to develop powerful and loving relationships with The Big Three and watch as you begin to create more of these memorable moments in your life.

You will thank yourself if you make it your mission to do so. For the day will come when you will be able to look back and say my life was a life well lived.

Unfortunately, in today's society, many of us can't remember what we did or ate two days ago, let alone remember all the great memories that we lived through at the end of our life. Because in today's society, many of us are lacking the power of purposeful and real relationships with others because we are lacking the will to keep our relationships with others alive. And the reason we are lacking the will to keep our relationships alive, is because we are lacking real depth within our relationships.

In other words, we are only scratching the surface of the relationships we have with others, all because we don't want to get hurt. You see, there is a whole other universe waiting to be seen inside the depths of the human being. Don't be afraid to scratch deeper than the surface, for what you might find is a universe waiting to be discovered.

For instance, have you ever talked to another person's soul? Have you ever connected so deeply to another person that each breath was in sync, each blink mimicked, and what you said was what they were going to say, and vice versa?

Being truly connected and diving into the depths of another person is what makes relationships so fun and exciting. When you become genuinely interested in other people, you will begin to understand what it is I am talking about. You two will begin to create the true connection that it takes to really create a purposeful and powerful relationship with one another.

Once you both become genuinely interested and decide to tear down the walls and uncover more than just what meets the eye, you'll begin to feel purpose in your life!

There have been so many times that my brother and I have had this powerful and deep connection between one another. Being in tune and genuinely interested in what it is he was talking about allowed us to deeply connect.

Deeply connecting with my brother are the moments I will never forget. But why are the moments with my brother more memorable than the moments I spend with the people whom I work with? Well, that is because of the connection and bond we have that awakens our souls every time we speak and dive deep into each other's life. We get curious about one another and ask in-depth questions that feed our souls natural curiosity. We spend hours in conversation.

The connection we have when we allow ourselves to fully let go and dive into one another's souls, is one of pure magic. You can experience this magic too, once you let go, and let yourself dive into the other's soul. Once you have arrived, you will begin to enter a place where time doesn't exist, where your attention is fully locked into their eyes, where your appreciation explodes for life because of your state of connection, and where your adoration of the conversation is unbreakable because of how your soul feels alive, listened to, felt and loved.

In this state of connection is when we become one with ourselves and the universe, for this is a place where time no longer exists. And only when we start to lose our focus, do we realize how much energy we burn through. These moments allow us to turn back to reality and realize that what seemed to be only minutes of conversation, turned into hours of in-depth, life-changing, and soul-staining conversation.

The best way to let people know that we hear them, is to make sure we are being a good listener and encourage them to talk more about what's important to them. This allows our souls to open up and become even more alive and free. Don't be afraid to scratch more than the surface. For what lies below the surface is a soul and a powerful and loving heart.

This world needs more purposeful relationships that supply each and every one of us with true love, deep connection, and the feeling of importance.

Go to the person you trust the most, let go and be vulnerable and start to experience what life has to offer when you fully engage in powerful and loving conversations. You have a whole life waiting for you to experience inside the depths of people whom you care about.

Be an explorer, an adventurer, a truth seeker and a truth

teller. We need this now more than ever, so don't be afraid to unlock your soul or another's. The truest way you can unlock your soul and cultivate purpose in your life is with another's soul. So, don't be afraid to unlock yours and live your fullest life by diving deep into the depths of another person.

You have a whole life waiting for you. The reason you should build powerful and loving relationships with others is to experience your spiritual life and a life full of love, memories, joy, purpose and connection.

HOW TO BUILD POWERFUL AND LOVING RELATIONSHIPS WITH OTHERS

In this section of the book, it is my goal to really help you figure out how you can become the perfect partner with the person you are in a relationship with, and create and enhance the level of joy, compassion, love, enjoyment and fun you feel, so that both of your needs and hearts desires are met at the highest level possible.

These chapters will help you build meaningful and deep relationships no matter what the relationship is like right now. These following chapters will help you improve the quality of your life and relationship you have, even if you already have an extraordinary relationship with the people that mean the most to you.

By integrating each one of these discoveries into your life, you will be able to dramatically improve and rekindle that flame that may have been lost.

17

CLEARING THE WAY TOWARD LOVE

> "It's not about creating an ordinary relationship. It's about creating an extraordinary relationship. In fact, it's about creating a truly magnificent relationship–the kind that is so full of joy, love, passion and excitement that it feels like a dream."
>
> — TONY ROBBINS

Throughout my entire life relationships have been rather disappointing and challenging. That is until I discovered a few foundational elements that have helped me to create a magnificent and fulfilling relationship.

Your deep inner joy in life depends on your ability to discover and deeply connect with another person and then be able to sustain and grow that relationship over the long term. Unfortunately, doing this successfully is one of life's greatest struggles. However, after reading through this book a few times and implementing the teachings that I will teach you, it won't be as difficult.

Who you choose as a partner can and will have a

profound impact on your joy in this lifetime. So, if you want to live a more joyful and fulfilling life following these next couple of steps will most definitely help you to achieve that.

STEP #1: Start with your vision in mind.

Your ability to select the right partner and to deeply connect with that person on all levels–physically, mentally, emotionally, and spiritually will directly affect your ability to create a long lasting, powerful and loving relationship with deep love for others.

If you are unsure how to select your right partner and unsure who is right for you, be sure to start with your vision in mind.

The first step to develop a long lasting, powerful and loving relationship with deep love is to create a vision for what it is you really want in and out of your relationship. Without understanding what it is your heart truly wants, you might find it very difficult to attract into your life the person who is best fit for you.

I don't want something that has a profound impact on your happiness to be difficult for you. I want to make it easy for you to get very clear on what it is you want so that you can have what your heart desires and live the life you truly want to live with the love you truly want to have in your life. That is why it is vitally important for you to answer the following questions right now.

THE QUESTIONS

What is it that you really want in your life and out of your next or current relationship? What is it that would light you up and excite you? What's your vison for what this relationship with your partner would create in the world that would inspire you to be in this relationship? Would it create an excitement and a joy that would keep your head held up so high you would never be afraid to love again? Would it create an everlasting fire within your heart to be the best person you could be?

Make your vision compelling to you, exciting and clear, so that you get so much emotion from your vision that you'll plant the burning desire within your heart to make it happen and find that special person.

Your vision of your ideal relationship will help you have the will to say yes to the right people and no to those relationships that no longer serve you. Knowing your vision will uncover your worth. Knowing your worth will make it easier for you to find that special someone! So, make your vision exciting and compelling.

Make it so exciting and compelling that your vision of your ideal relationship inspires you and motivates you to have the courage needed in order to put yourself out there. Take action, better yourself, and make it come true. Tony Robbins has said, "The first step toward anything you want is to decide what's your vision for what you really want. You can't make something happen until you get very clear on what it is you want."

It is going to be rather hard to make something come true and manifest into your life if you are unclear about your vision. That is why it is so very important to focus on creating a compelling vision because without a vision, people perish.

You need to start to create a vision for your relationship. This vision should be directed toward what is it you really want most in your life. What would bring you the most joy? What would light your heart on fire with love? What does this relationship look like and feel like when you are with them?

Be sure to go in depth with it and uncover what the person will look like and act like. What values do they have, what is the vision in your heart telling you this relationship would create in the world that would inspire you to be in that relationship with them? Because here is the thing, without a vision of what the relationship is going to be like, you're going to settle for whatever shows up in your life that looks half good. Don't do this to yourself. Be kind enough to yourself to only receive what you deserve to have. Deep down you know your worth and you also know how you should be treated.

Quit settling and start creating a higher standard and vision for yourself so that you can create and have the powerful and loving relationship your heart truly deserves.

18

BUILDING THE VISION FOR YOUR RELATIONSHIP

> " "You are the architect of your own destiny; you are the master of your own fate; you are behind the steering wheel of your life. There are no limitations to what you can do, have, or be. Accept the limitations you place on yourself by your own thinking."
>
> — Brian Tracy

Throughout my visit here on Earth, I have met many people who seem to hate their life. They hate their nine-to-five job; they complain about the relationship they are in with their significant other; they complain about the weather; they complain about how their car or cell phone is not good enough and how they dislike their house or where they live.

They are annoyed by their family and irritated with their boss at work; they complain about other people daily, stress about finances, and every miserable thing that has happened in their life is of course somebody else's fault but their own. I feel sorry for these people because I believe that they are people who had hopes, dreams and aspirations to do great things in their life, and somehow their life just isn't going as they planned it would if they even planned it out at all.

They are living with disappointment and frustration in themselves and living an unfulfilling life. As sad as this may be, I am here to give you some great news! I believe that every person has the ability to be the architect of their own life, or at least harnesses the power within themselves to be the architect of their life as long as they are ready to be. Being the architect of your own life means that you are in the driver's seat, behind the steering wheel, with your foot on the gas pedal making your way confidently, courageously and faithfully through life.

In this life, you have the ability to make it a great one if you take one hundred percent full responsibility for your life like you do when you drive a car. Just like you are in control of certain things in your life, like your attitude and what type of action you take. You are also in control of the type of relationships you will develop and keep in your life. You have the ability to create beautiful and loving relationships in your life as long as you take the second step of the process seriously.

The second part to building a powerful and loving relationship with others is to decide that you are capable of creating your own relationship. You have control over every choice that you make and every relationship that you are in. If you're in a miserable job or relationship, you have the ability to create a strategy to leave your miserable relationship or job and find one that you actually love.

If you're in a miserable relationship with someone you love you have the ability to change that. If you have a verbally abusive friend, you have the choice to stop being friends. If you have a poor life and mindset, you have the ability and power within you to change that too.

Your life and relationships are as enjoyable and loving as you decide to create them to be. If you believe in yourself and take daily action, you can begin to create the life and relationship of your dreams. You just have to be willing to put in the work, believe in yourself and always be willing to do what is necessary for you to have the life and relationships you want to have.

The path toward creating that relationship your heart truly desires might not be the easiest, but it will be a path that is worth taking. If you are ready to build the relationships you have always wanted to have, here is what I have learned to do in order to attract the beautiful relationships I have in my life.

I want you to be able to experience the joy and fulfillment I am so grateful to receive when I am around my friends, family, lover and business team. These relationships I have created in my life are ones that have opened so many doors that are continuously leading me toward financial abundance, support, love, joy, memories and fulfillment. They are relationships that are built on true friendship and meaning.

STEP #2: Create a list of what you want, what you must not have, and who you must become to attract that relationship.

When you have clarity of intention, the universe conspires with you to make it come true. Creating extreme clarity is so vital when it comes to creating the life and relationships your heart and soul truly desires. If you're in a relationship already, you should still know where you want to steer your ship. If you're single, this will help you weed through all the mess a lot more.

If you want a stronger relationship with yourself, others, or God you must begin to create extreme clarity toward what you want those relationships to look and feel like. You need a vision of what you want in detail in terms of your emotional, physical, spiritual, and mental desires.

Today, I want you to be bold enough to ask the universe

for what it is your heart truly wants. And be courageous enough to take a stand for what it is your heart truly desires. Taking the time to create a list will be super beneficial for you and will help you to find who and what you are looking for. If you don't know what you want, you just might end up with someone who isn't right for you.

Let's get this part of our lives right by taking the time needed to write down what it is you want and what it is you must not have in your relationships so that you don't end up in a relationship you regret getting into.

Writing down what you must not have in your relationship is so very important to do. It will help you to avoid the people who are not good for you and your needs. The only way to know what it is you truly want in life is to have an awareness of what it is you don't want. This list that you are going to create should consist of the things you don't want this person to be.

When you look at your answers to the following questions it might seem impossible to achieve. But when you answer the very last question, chances are you will step into your greatest self and begin to live a better quality of life and attract that person you want to attract. And that really helps because it takes the focus off of looking for the one, to being the one.

Spend some time today and carefully think through and answer these questions. I want you to sit down and be an artist and paint a picture of what it is you want and don't want in your life. Don't just give one-word answers or list a few words out. Describe in great detail what it is you want and don't want.

THE QUESTIONS

What do I want to experience in my relationship? How do I want to be treated? How do I want to show up? How does it feel to be around this person when I am with them? What do we do when we are together? Who do I really need in my life? What do they do on their own time without me? Who are they as a person right now? (Do not be confused with their hire potential.

Everyone has a crazy amount of potential. You need to see if they show the quality of the person who is currently striving to be their best self as well.) What are your absolute requirements and standards? What are their standards? What is their view on children? How do they want to raise their children? What are their views on money? Are they a carefree spender, saver, or investor? What's their relationship like with their family and friends? What's their health like? What type of friends do they have? Are they inspiring and positive or closed off and negative? What types of foods do they not eat? What types of movies do they not like to watch? What types of music do they not like to listen to? What do you see them doing in their free time? Are they impacting others to live a better quality of life or watching Netflix and playing video games? Are they someone who likes to fight, argue and be right or are they someone who likes to listen, be patient and forgive? What do I refuse to tolerate? What will I never put up with? What are the red flags and deal breakers no matter what?

The choice is yours. You get to create your reality and relationships you have. There is no right or wrong answer. You just need to know what it is you want and what it is you don't want. This will be a massive game changer. Lastly, you need to know the kind of person who you need to become so that you can attract your powerful and loving relationship. So, who do you need to become to appear attractive to that person who you just described?

19

PAY ATTENTION

66 "To build a powerful relationship with those whom mean the most to you, give them these three things: attention, appreciation and adoration."

— TYLER JOE STRATTON

Attention is the most basic form of love that anyone can give at any time. When we give our attention, we give our love, and when we give our love, we bless those who we give it to. We become blessed to be able to feel and give it to those who are receiving it. Giving what you want to receive will set your life and relationship up for success, love, and joy.

There is such a major challenge today when it comes to your attention, and if you want to learn to have a powerful and loving relationship with others, the first A cannot be looked over. Think about all the things in life that need your attention. Your pet, your customers, yourself, plants, others etc. Anything that lives needs attention from someone or something. Think about it: in order to be kept strong, a relationship must be attended to regularly, just like a plant.

Your relationship doesn't need constant attention, but it does need regular and proper attention in order for it to grow into something strong and beautiful. If you look over the first A, and not give that special rose flower your regular attention, it will wither away after a while of not being given what it needs.

If you neglect this precious flower for too long, then no matter how much water you give it, or how much quality care you show it, it is not coming back. Always make it your purpose to give your time and attention to those you love and to those you care about.

For if you show attention to others, take care of them, and show them your love, you will receive what you've sown. Let that be a lesson you take into every relationship you find yourself in. Be a giver, not a taker! It's not what's in it for me, it's what can I do to better serve them.

I know so many people who cannot pay attention to a great movie let alone give their attention to another person and be in a conversation or connect with others. I was actually one of those people who couldn't give my attention to others.

I remember a time when I told my brother in New York City, how afraid I was to go out and explore the different social restaurants and comedy clubs with him. Before entering the comedy club, I was overwhelmed with social anxiety. I was so afraid I would have to hold a conversation with a random stranger.

Being an introvert and not always enjoying socializing with many people, I knew I had to stretch myself to talk and connect with others. I remember asking him before we got out of the taxicab that night, "How do I talk to someone who I have no common interests with? What do I do then?" The advice he gave me helped me a lot, and I figure it's only right for me to share this advice with you.

You see, before we went out to the comedy club that night, he reminded me that when talking to someone, the one thing he said to do was just pay attention and keep my eyes engaged with them. Pay close attention to what they have to say, for people don't care what you have to say, they only care about your attention you give them while they are talking to you.

Paying attention will take you far in life and help you create a deeper connection with anyone you meet. Paying attention and being an active listener will really help the person you are listening to feel like they had the best conversation with you because you sat there listening and gave them your attention.

Once I learned that all people really want is my full attention, I made it my intention that night to focus on giving my attention to those I would go out and talk to. Paying attention was the focus for the night, and let me tell you, I hit it off with so many amazing people without saying more than a few dozen words.

I felt like we were profoundly connecting, and to be honest, I felt more connected in that moment than I have ever felt in a very long time. Giving your full attention to someone will genuinely help you overcome that feeling of loneliness or that feeling of being disconnected.

If your relationship is lacking because you can't seem to connect with your partner, it might be because you are not giving your full attention to your partner. Don't miss out on amazing people and conversation because you are afraid of what others might think of you. There are too many great people out there who have amazing stories and connections who might be able to help you sometime down the road when you need someone. **The world is only as lonely and disconnected as you make it.**

There are so many people who are missing out on deeply connected relationships with others and an amazing life full of beauty and wonder because they can't connect to anyone anymore. They can't keep their eyes on each other long enough to pay attention to each other without looking around at everything else that is going on around them, or they keep checking their phone every five minutes.

There is nothing more unsexy than being in a conversation with someone, especially when it's your significant other, who all of the sudden looks at their phone and stops paying attention to you. How disconnected do you feel when someone does that to you while you are talking to them? It drives me nuts! And that is one of the challenges we all face today in our relationships.

It doesn't take much to have an outstanding and influential relationship with yourself or others. All it takes is some attention. If you feel like you have lost the spark in your relationship and life, be sure to give your life and relationships more of your sincere and meaningful attention and watch the spark begin to ignite into a beautiful connection and deep relationship once again.

BE FULLY PRESENT

What does it take to really take your relationship with others to the next level? It takes a mentality shift that will make your intention become your attention for people.

To be in a strong and powerful relationship with someone else, you really need to learn to bring your energetic presence and be right there with them totally absorbed in the NOW. Be fully present, look deep into their eyes and be engaged in every word that they speak.

Find a way to bring that moment alive by bringing the enthusiasm while paying attention to them. Be enthusiastic towards the relationship that you are in with them, be excited for the moment and the connection you have the privilege to share with that person. For what you are really doing in that moment is sharing life with one another!

Another tactic you can use to help take your relationship

to the next level is learn to read their body language. By paying attention to their body language, you can learn to sense the type of energy that they are giving off and what they might need from you. You might need to bring the joy, the love, and the inspiration, or you might need to bring the empathy, hugs, and feelings to them.

You can receive a lot when you begin to pay full attention to them and their body language. I promise you, that if you can bring to the moment that they are after, then the connection and relationship you have with your partner, spouse, wife, husband, lover, boyfriend, girlfriend, friend or stranger will make you stand out and make them feel grateful to be with you and so thankful that you are there with them and for them!

The greatest gift you can give someone is your attention. That's one of the main ingredients that everyone has been wanting from you. They have been seeking out the type of attention that makes them know they matter and are cared for.

You have the ability to fully connect and really build powerful and loving relationships if you just stay present in this moment with them. Being fully present with them will help them to feel special. Be there and pay attention because like Jesse Jackson said a long time ago, "People don't want your presents, they want your presence." Meaning they don't want your gifts or your things, they just want you, and all of you; powerfully engaged and connected with them again.

If you are going to develop a stronger and more loving relationship, or any type of positive relationship in your life, then you will want to improve your attention. For great relationships will come into your life from your ability to improve your attention and presence.

Give the gift of your presence to that person who is in that moment with you. Be vitally there and present with them again. Put down your phone when you are with them, for your phone is not what will matter in the end. Your phone is not what you are going to remember when you sit back to reflect on the life you have lived. **It is the relationships you have with others that you will remember and what will truly matter in the end**. So, do yourself, your life and the person you are with a favor and put down your phone. Don't pick it up when you are with that person, unless it is an emergency.

A life without your phone is a life that can be peaceful, joyful, exciting and wonderful. Learn to have fun exploring who that person truly is at heart. Be curious! Life has a very special gift to offer you if you are willing to drop your distractions and give your full attention to that human being who is in that moment with you.

You will never give to get nothing in return and when you give someone your full attention, life will offer aliveness, fun, excitement and memories. Life is waiting for you to experience what it has to offer, but you must learn to free yourself from the distractions and learn to pay attention to the wonderful gift of life others can offer you.

Think about it for a moment; your best memories are not found or made when you keep your head down and focused on your phone. Those are just moments that waste your life away as the time continually ticks your life away.

The best memories of your life will probably have to do with the relationships you have had in your life. They were the times when the two of you or a group of you were just totally absorbed in the moment together. The times you will remember are the times that are memorable. They were the times your dad took you fishing or hunting. They were the times you would cook the Thanksgiving turkey at your grandmother's house with your family. They were the times where you held a fun backyard football game with your family and friends. They were the times you were all at the dinner table laughing so hard your stomach was in pain and the tears would not stop rolling out of your eyes. Those are the moments you don't want to miss.

Your life is as powerful as your memories. If you want to create a wonderful life, you must begin to create wonderful memories. It's your memories of being surrounded by people who care, love, serve, and bring joy that create a life worth remembering.

These are the memories where life becomes fully lived and vibrantly experienced because of the wonderful connection you all had in that very special present moment together. Life is about experiencing these wonderful moments, and they will be offered to you more frequently if you just learn to pay attention to others more often by being someone who stays in the present moment.

In order to live a life to its fullest, you must understand that you must be able to give a powerful amount of attention to those in your life that make it meaningful.

Without the ability to pay attention to yourself and to others, you will start to increase all the sicknesses that happen to you and in your relationships. Think about this for a moment; when you stop paying attention to yourself or to others, you start to beat yourself up, and the relationship you have with yourself and others start to fall apart.

Over a long period of time, if you do not pay attention, you will find yourself without that special someone in your life, or worse, fired from a job or with some kind of illness or disease.

Being able to pay attention is the ability to take care of yourself and others. Pay more attention, and you begin to collect many more moments in your life that you can enjoy and cherish. Don't let life slip away because you haven't been paying any attention to it or others. Start paying attention and be gifted with the beauty of memories and with powerful and loving relationships with those who matter.

20

GIVE APPRECIATION

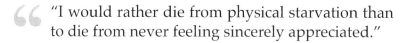

"I would rather die from physical starvation than to die from never feeling sincerely appreciated."

— Tyler Joe Stratton

There is one fundamental law that stands apart from all other requirements in regard to human conduct. It's a law that if we obey, we will rarely find ourselves getting into trouble.

If we follow this law, it has the potential to give us the relationships our hearts indeed desire and the deep inner joy that we all crave. But the very moment we decide to break this law, we all shall find ourselves lost, lonely, and broken.

The law is this: *Always make the other person feel appreciated.* William James once said, "The deepest principle in human nature is the craving to be appreciated." If you ever find yourself in a relationship where your relationship is losing the spark it once had, one of the best plans of action you can take is to give honest and sincere appreciation to your partner.

Throughout human history, there has been one essential universal rule that has evolved throughout thousands of years that we all must follow to live a productive life. This law was taught to me in grade school, and it is one that I will never forget.

It is a law that I still do my best to live by daily and has been the secret to my inner joy, peace, and love that lives within me. It is a law that Confucius preached to his followers in China centuries ago. Lao-tse, the founder of Taoism, taught it to his disciples in the Valley of the Han. Buddha preached it on the bank of the Holy Ganges five hundred years before Christ. The sacred books of Hinduism taught it a thousand years before that, and Jesus taught it in Judea over two thousand years ago.

However, Jesus summed it up very nicely and has become one of the most important rules we must all learn to live by in this world: "Do unto others as you would have others do unto you." If we could all live by what is called the Golden Rule, our lives would dramatically change.

For if we could make common sense, common practice and implement the Golden Rule into our lives, we would begin to discover a deep inner peace first within ourselves and then within the world.

We all want the approval of those who we surround ourselves. We are all searching for significance and to be recognized as great humans. We all want to feel as though we are essential and are genuinely appreciated. So, if you're going to begin to achieve greatness in your life and your relationships, you must start to follow the Golden Rule, and give unto others what we would have others give unto us. Make this your everyday mission and watch your life, and relationships begin to improve for the better.

Did you know that a person's greatest emotional need is to feel appreciated? Did you know that seventy percent of employees say that they would leave their job and lose their security just because they didn't feel appreciated enough? Do you understand just how valuable it is to make another person feel seen, heard, felt or more importantly appreciated?

It could make someone's day, change a life or even save a life, so why not give more appreciation to the ones we love and to those with whom we are in a relationship with? Well, my thought, is because many of us are just too lazy and lack the ambition to work hard for the things we want the most.

People leave relationships all the time because they no longer feel appreciated. If you could leave yourself, I am sure you would. I know there are times in my life where I would have loved to have left myself. I am sure you have found yourself in the same sinking boat as I have. For example, have you ever said to yourself, "Man, I wish I could just leave this town or this place and just get away?" If so, these are the moments where you are trying to escape from what seems to be the situation, but in truth, it is just you trying to escape from yourself.

It is you trying to escape your thoughts and emotions that are causing you an issue. If we could leave ourselves, I am sure many of us would. Being left behind, or just left alone, seems to be an issue we all have to face at least once in our lives. However, you can learn to avoid that feeling and learn to live your fullest life once you start to appreciate yourself and the people you are with.

I don't mean just appreciating them in a small insignificant way like, "Hey, I appreciate you doing x, y, or z for me." Although that is great, it won't take your relationship or life to the next level.

Getting to the next level and living your fullest life with those that are in your life, will take a massive amount of courage to begin to open your hurting heart and appreciate people on a whole new and deeper level.

To be grateful, you need to learn to open up your heart and come from a place of kindness, truth, and compassion. Learning to open your heart up, without the fear of getting hurt, will help you appreciate everything about them from the struggles they are facing to the overall life they are living.

But while doing so, you must not forget yourself in the process of helping others, for you need to learn to love and to appreciate yourself while caring for others. If you don't water your own heart, mind, soul, and body, you will find it hard to help others in a way that shows them you truly appreciate the challenges they are facing; their dark moments, their frustrations, all the things that you might find stupid, and all the things that might drive you insane.

Learn to love to appreciate it all. I know this could be challenging for some of you like it was for me, but it can be made a lot easier by recognizing that all people are unique in their way. Recognizing their uniqueness will help you see that they are one of a kind and very rare. Realizing there is no one in the world like them will open your eyes, and hopefully your heart, enough so that you can begin to see the truth and how precious they indeed are.

Once you appreciate who and what they are, you will start to treat them more like a diamond rather than a rock. Rarity is treated differently than regularity, and everyone is very rare. So, all should be appreciated.

To begin to appreciate their uniqueness and see how that person is very special, create a list of the things that make them special and allow yourself to focus in on their uniqueness. Once you recognize their uniqueness and how special they are, continue to open your heart and come from a place of kindness and compassion. Come from a place of heart not hurt!

When coming from this place of kindness and compassion, you will pay more attention and appreciate their struggle and their life a little bit deeper. While giving more awareness and appreciation to their conflict and their life, what you might find is an appreciation for your own life. You will begin to realize just how grateful you are for being strong enough to be able to help them get through what they are going through and be thankful that you are not going through what it is they are. And because you appreciate just that and are coming from your heart, you can offer your best advice from a place of kindness and compassion that will help you provide the helping hand they may be seeking.

A helping hand is a happy hand that is ready to give unto others and that willingness to give unto others will lead you to a happier you! You can set yourself up to experience powerful and loving relationships, and even more fabulous memories when you learn to appreciate others and yourself.

To understand, and to truly appreciate someone, is to accept who they are on a level that they have never felt accepted before. In a world where judgement rules the mind and everyone has a say in what you are wearing, doing, who you are with or not with, and everything else under the sun, learning to appreciate someone on a level where they have never felt accepted will help them to become more themselves. It will help them unlock their heart, to allow the love that they so rightfully deserve back in.

This world can sometimes seem as if it is in a dark place, and the hope for humanity might seem to be darker than it is bright, to some of you. However, if you can appreciate someone at a level where they have never felt accepted and appreciated, then they will take that feeling and pass it on to another. They will then pass it on to another, and then another, and so on.

We can change this world just by the appreciation we give to another. To really show someone that we appreciate them, is to act from a place called "kindness". Actor, Morgan Freeman, was once asked, "How do we change the world?" His response was, "One random act of kindness at a time."

If we learn to appreciate others, we hold the raw power to truly begin to leave our mark on the world and begin to make it a better place than which we found it. And in order for us to reach the place where they have never felt accepted before, we have to appreciate their soul! You have to learn to appreciate them for who they are as a human being and learn to accept them with true respect and appreciation.

The appreciation you show them must go deeper than just showing them how much you appreciate them with a gift. You see, in today's world, many of us try to show how much we appreciate someone with the gifts we buy them, but that only scratches the surface, and they can't take that gift to the grave with them.

Give them something they can take to the grave. Something that impacts their soul so deeply that they will remember it for two lifetimes. Show them how special they are by appreciating their humanity. Show them how appreciated they are for their reality, and not just what they may have done for you.

In order to appreciate someone's whole reality, the first step you can take when around someone is to first encourage them to talk more about themselves. Everyone loves to talk about themselves.

If you can encourage someone to talk about themselves and do some deep listening, they will begin to feel much more appreciated. You can do this by asking questions that will get them talking about their life and their day. Learning to hold a conversation during the times your significant other or someone is talking to you is vital, but getting them to really express more about what they are talking about will show them how much you appreciate them.

For example, In John Gray's book, Men are From Mars and Women Are from Venus, he states, "You should know the questions you are going to ask your partner when they come home from work or in your communications." He goes on to explain that there are things that you can say to your woman or your man, or to another person which will really help them feel more appreciated.

So, coming up with a list of things you can say to appreciate someone's reality, is a game and life changer. This will really help them feel more appreciated and help you both to grow and develop a powerful and loving relationship with each other.

Here are a few examples that you can start incorporating into your life right now to help make someone feel appreciated.

The next time you and your significant other, or anyone for that matter, comes up to you and starts telling you about their day or the things that are troubling them, show them that you appreciate them and show them they are being listened to by saying, "Tell me more about that," or "What else happened?" Stating this powerful phrase to someone while they are talking to you, will light their soul on fire. For when you ask people to give you more information, what you really are doing is giving them the power to express and communicate more deeply, the things they believe are important to them.

When talking to someone who wants to listen to you, it will really help that person who is being listened to feel more listened to, more empathetic, more respected, more understood, and make them feel more appreciated and loved. This will help the connection between the two of you grow so much deeper.

Another one that I seem to use when I am around people who complain about anything and everything, is to try to empathize with them by saying, "Wow, that is a bummer. I am sorry you are going through or experiencing that." Listening is such an important skill to learn. However, so is learning to empathize with someone who is complaining about their day.

Learn to master both and you will have the power to create powerful and loving relationships with anyone. There are plenty of people who love to drop their bad news on your lap. When someone drops their bad news or bad day luggage on your lap, make sure to bring your heart to the conversation and put yourself in their shoes. Feel the stress, worry, sadness or trouble that they are experiencing, and then you will know exactly what to say.

Putting yourself in their shoes will help you not feel so annoyed by all the negativity. Being able to feel what they feel and say the right thing is important to do during these times. It can either ignite a bigger fire or extinguish it into a peace of mind.

Being able to put yourself in their shoes and empathize with them, will help them feel more important and sense your sincerity. That is so important for someone to hear and feel when they are experiencing a low time in their day or life. So, do both you and your partner a favor by being there with them in their time of need. For when you are, the gift you will receive is one that will make you feel proud of being you.

The last thing I do, that makes others feel so appreciated and heard, is to say, "I am here with you and for you. Is there anything I can do?" Coming from a place of service is what you can do anytime someone is seeking your attention. I know many of you feel interrupted when someone is seeking your attention, especially when they want to share their negative thoughts and emotions with you. However, by pushing yourself to the side for a moment and by coming from a place of love and service, it will become such a powerful experience for you and for the person who needs you and your attention.

This is so powerful to do, and it can really help someone who is looking for help or feeling alone or just frustrated. The next time humanity calls upon you and someone is there seeking your attention, be a person of love and service.

Remember, in order to really build a powerful and loving relationship with another, you must show them how much you appreciate them by truly and deeply, feeling and sensing the things in which they are feeling and sensing in that moment. Share your best self with them by showing them how much you appreciate them by being someone who gives them meaningful and real compliments that show them how much you care.

Meaningful and real compliments can take your relationship to the next level. For when you say something that is very true and aligns with who they truly believe they are and what they did, they will feel the true joy that appreciation can bring to anyone. Happiness will never fulfill the hearts of those who never take the time to appreciate what they have in front of them. The more you appreciate in your life, the happier you will be for the rest of your life!

21

ADORATION

66 "The grandest ambition that any man can possibly have is to so live and so improve himself in heart and brain as to be worthy of the love of some splendid woman; and the grandest ambition of any girl is to make herself worthy of the love and adoration of some magnificent man."

— ROBERT GREEN INGERSOLL

D o you want a powerful and loving relationship? Most people do but are too lazy to put in the work and commitment to create what it is they want. Yet no matter how hard they try, many people still struggle to find a powerful and loving relationship, or they struggle to create one with their partner. Why is this so hard for many of us?

The reason that most of us in this world have no idea what actually creates a powerful and loving relationship with another is because many have no one to look up to. There is no prime example that they can reach out to and look to for help. Many people no longer have a relationship to look up to because their parents didn't have a clue on how to keep a powerful and loving relationship, and their parents and role models didn't have a clue.

I believe that one of the biggest reasons why many of us do not have other relationships to look up to is because many of these relationships lose their aliveness, vibrancy, and more importantly, adoration over the long term.

We have a problem and sometimes the problem is that we don't adore the person that we are with after being with them for a while. By the time you were born, many parents are normally out of the state of pure passion and adoration for one another. We become their love, and they start to lose the meaningful love and connection they used to have for one another or for themselves.

Now, I am not saying this about everyone out there. I still have family members who are madly in love after thirty years of being married. However, what I am saying is that many of us experience the downfall of the relationship between our parents or those who we grow up with. Because of this downfall, we stop seeing what adoration and love looks like, and therein lies my next point.

In order to build a powerful and loving relationship, you must learn to adore your lover and be open to loving others again. You have to resummon your ability to adore the one you are with and rekindle the love that still lives inside of you.

To resummon anything is normally very tough. So tough, that many don't really try it, or they have a massive amount of negativity in their mind and heart before they do try it once again. For instance, have you ever broken a habit and tried to get back into that habit? Have you ever stopped going to the gym and found it super hard to get back to the gym? Or have you ever had that one cookie that isn't in your diet and you can't seem to get back on your diet? I am sure many of you have, and because we have failed at resummoning up whatever we stopped doing, we have a lack of belief in ourselves.

The same goes for relationships. You have to start looking for the things in your lover or others which will light up that fire of adoration again. Feeling adored by others is such an amazing feeling, especially when it is by those you love and care about.

The way to adore others again is to set your focus on the first two A's; Appreciation and Attention. If you want your relationship to come back to life and upgrade your relationship from ordinary to extraordinary, you must give them more appreciation and show them more attention in order to show them how much you adore them.

When you give someone more attention and more appreciation, you will notice how much more alive and energetically powerful your relationship with that person will be. Your relationship with them will then become more alive and vibrant.

The love that was fading away and the doubtful thoughts that started to crowd your mind will start to leave, and love will show its wild and fun self again. When you start to adore the person you are with, and start to adore those who surround you, you will see their own uniqueness and you will notice that you will come from a place of service more often, and do more things for your lover and for others. It's a beautiful concept.

If you really want to generate love into your life by building powerful and loving relationships, then you will start supporting who they are and the dreams in which they are chasing. You will begin to treat them the same way you treated them when you first met them or started dating.

The spark that you might be lacking can be generated once again if that is what your heart truly desires. Get out of your own way and be there to help others enjoy life. Helping others enjoy their life will help you enjoy yours. When you constantly support and cheer on the individuals you are involved with, you will inevitably increase the overall joy you both want to experience. In the words of a proverb, "Help your brother's boat across, and your own will reach the shore." Another way I have heard it said before has been found in an old adage which I believe to this very day is still true: if you help enough people get what they want and feel the way they want to feel, you will automatically get what you want.

So, how have you been doing in this area of your own life? Have you been supporting others in a way that expresses to them that you are proud of who they are and who they are becoming? How are you doing with supporting their dreams they are chasing? Are you encouraging them to continue on or are you being their biggest critic? If you know that you can step up your game, then I suggest you do so.

If you really want to build that powerful and loving relationship with others, you really just need to step out of your own way and learn to ask yourself, "What can I do to serve them in a powerful way that can support what they love to do?"

Adoration is really about being of service to another and showing them how much you support the things that they truly enjoy doing. Adoration is about truly taking care of another. It is about wanting to see someone you care about be as successful and joyful as they can be. It's about helping them get there and reach a new level of joy, love, and success.

When you fully adore someone, what you will notice is just how desperately you want to see them happy and fully alive. When you really adore someone, you step out of your way and do whatever you can to make their life run a little more smoothly. Can you imagine a world where each person truly and fully adores one other person? Can you imagine what this world might look like if we could learn to focus on others just a little more deeply and personally? I know I can, and in hopes of our future, I hope that you start to live by these three A's (attention, appreciation, and adoration), and start living your fullest life by building powerful and loving relationships with these powerful tools.

22

THE POWER OF LETTING GO OF EXPECTATIONS

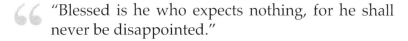 "Blessed is he who expects nothing, for he shall never be disappointed."

— ALEXANDER POPE

Shakespeare once said, "I always feel happy, you know why? Because I don't expect anything from anyone, expectations always hurt. Life is short, so love your life. Be happy and keep smiling. Just live for yourself, and before you speak, listen. Before you write, think. Before you spend, earn. Before you pray, forgive. Before you hurt, feel. Before you hate, love. Before you quit, try. Before you die, live." What a beautiful lesson. If you can live by this alone, your overall quality of life and relationships will increase drastically.

The lesson here is that you must learn to let go of the expectations that you set for yourself and for others if you want a powerful, loving and open relationship. Lots of people set too many expectations in their life which results in many relationships being in a constant battle due to the simple fact that they expect more from their partner and appreciate less, when in reality they should expect less and appreciate more.

Do you find yourself in a constant battle with your pets when you get home, like you do with your significant other, your family, or the person you live with? Probably not.

Let's take a dog for example, when you arrive home, how often do you hear yourself sigh or find yourself thinking about all the expectations your dog has for you once you get home? Probably never. Have you ever wondered just how great it is to come home to your puppy who holds no expectations whatsoever when you walk through that door? I know I sure have. It is so crazy just how much love and connection you feel right away when you see your dog wagging its tail, looking up at you with pure joy and love.

I am sure you feel a lot of love and a lot of appreciation as well as connection as soon as you walk through your door. I bet some of you even go home excited to feel love from your dog, due to the lack of connection and lack of love you experienced most of the day. Why is that? I believe the main reason we enjoy coming home to our dogs is because your dog never has any expectations for you once you get home. Your dog just simply and effortlessly accepts you for everything you are or are not without judgement. You could walk into your home and be having the worst day ever and be in a slump, with negative thoughts about your day running through your mind, only to affect your day in a negative manner.

However, no matter what you are going through, your dog is right there fully accepting you for who you are and what you are not. Why? Because your dog simply loves and accepts you without any expectations.

Just like a dog, you must learn to let go of all expectations towards others. You must learn to judge others the same way you would judge a tree as you are driving down the road; by not judging it at all. You don't judge trees, and you don't judge your dog. You either accept them and love them as they are, or do not accept them and love them as they are, so you let them go.

You must take this lesson and learn to do the same with people in order to develop a strong and powerful relationship with whoever it is you are trying to build a better relationship with. For when our expectations are not met, the mindless bickering and arguing starts to take effect, our feelings get crushed and we find ourselves in a miserable mood.

All this pain and misery takes hold, all because an expectation or a story in which you told yourself, and attached yourself to, was not met. After a long period of time of being hurt because of someone not meeting our expectations, we find ourselves separating from the one great connection we had in the beginning.

The more you expect from others, and the more you don't receive what you expected, the greater the stress and frustration you will face. There are many conscious and unconscious demands that you believe you need from someone in order to feel a certain way. It is your job to decipher what it is that you really want or need from that person and understand why you feel like you need it from them and not yourself.

Anytime I find myself pointing my finger and blaming the other person for whatever it is I believe is their fault, I keep perspective and always remind myself that there are four other fingers pointing back at me.

In the beginning of my first real relationship, I remember expecting my significant other to know how I felt about going out to a party, or how I felt about something that came up. I just figured she knew what I expected from her. However, what I learned as I got older and wiser, was the fact that the person I was expecting something from, didn't even know what it was that I was expecting.

For some weird reason, I thought that she could read and understand my mind and the vibe or energy that I was putting out there without speaking to her clearly and directly. As you can imagine this never ended well, and it didn't do anything besides cause more frustration and arguments that just gave us another reason to leave one another.

Often the reason why the person you are expecting something from doesn't know what it is you are expecting of them is because you may not be aware of what it is you want or why you want what you want is so important to you.

Understanding the deeper reason why you expect them to do something or be a certain way will help you communicate clearly to them what it is you are after. You must become clear and understand the reason why you want what it is you want from others. Be willing to let go of whatever the outcome might be. Some of the expectations that I seem to place on others are listed below.

"So and so" should have: known better than to do that, helped me out more, been there for me, said this, liked me, loved me, been happier, been more grateful, not have made the same mistakes twice, made me feel more loved, or not have said that in front of my family.

We all have different expectations for the different relationships we develop in our lives. When those people who are involved in our lives are not living up to our expectations, thoughts and wishes, the end result is always the same for many of us; disappointment lingers in our hearts and minds, followed by feelings of frustration, anger, hurt, resentment, sadness and insignificance. This all adds up to a life full of stress and living negatively.

Doesn't sound like a life well lived, does it? Life is too valuable and too short to get upset with those who don't meet our expectations, for it is us who loses in the end. Just like Kris Allen's song Live Like We're Dying states,

We only got 86 400 seconds in a day
To turn it all around or to throw it all away

Gotta tell 'em that we love 'em while we got the chance
to say,
Gotta live like we're dying, oh.

Don't waste any more of the 86,400 seconds that are in the day by holding on to expectations that might only lead you to feel frustrated and hurt. The faster you can let go of the expectations you hold over yourself, your life, or someone's head, the faster you will begin to feel more peaceful and liberated.

That is why I ask you to open your mind and your heart to realize that the moment you place an expectation on someone else is the moment you have created a belief and a story in which you have committed your mind to believing.

You have set yourself up to lose and to feel the pain and frustration. The truth is, the only person who you should be putting expectations on is yourself. But even when you find yourself doing this, don't be too hard on yourself if you don't meet your own expectations.

For you can drown yourself heavily if you don't live up to them. So instead of finding yourself struggling to swim, remind yourself to live like you are dying and begin to move through the problem by figuring out why you didn't meet what you expected to.

Then let go of it and replace it with appreciation. This way of thinking, and this way of action taking, has gotten me further in life than beating myself up for not meeting the expectations I expected to.

Something we must realize is that we cannot control everything, and that we cannot make everything we want to come true. Sometimes we must learn to let go and let God guide us onto the correct path. God knows the way, even when we don't.

You see, I expected to be a Division one athlete and keep

my football career alive. However, truth be told, after my injury and many long nights of questioning what it is I should do and what choice I should choose, I decided to let go of the expectation of becoming a division one athlete and let God take over for a little while. I allowed God to take control and put my trust in Him. Everything seemed to work out.

Letting go and letting God take control of my life was a very hard thing for me to do. But while I continued to let go and let God pray and sit in silence, I found my faith strengthened and eventually found my next path.

Now I am a life coach, an author, a speaker, a business owner, and a much better person today than I was back then. I am grateful; I am loving; I am caring, and I am happy to know who I am and what I stand for. I am so much more than I expected to be.

Although letting go of my expectations was super challenging, I promise you that letting go of them will be worth it. I am telling you that your expectations will limit you and hurt you, while your appreciation toward yourself, others, and God as well as your ability to let go will help you to become limitless and live your fullest life.

Don't hide behind your expectations and don't let your expectations control the quality of life you live. You are limitless; you are strong, and you are so much more than what you expect yourself to be, for something greater is on your side.

So, don't be afraid to let go of the expectations and stories you are holding on to. What is on the other end of letting go and letting God in, is a life waiting to be fully lived. Don't waste another minute. Don't damage your thoughts and ruin your emotions. Don't let your expectations take another day away from the life you have been gifted with. Begin to make the switch of your expectations with appreciation and gratitude!

23

THE IMPORTANCE OF YOUR TIME AND YOUR WORD

> "Time is the currency of relationships. If you want to invest into your relationships, start by investing your time."
>
> — DAVE WILLIS

The greatest gift you will ever give to another person is not your money or material things, it is your time. In order to build a powerful and loving relationship with others, you must realize that no amount of money can purchase happiness, extra years, months, weeks, days, hours, or minutes.

Your time is an extremely precious commodity and you must begin to use it wisely. Harvey Mackay, Author of *Swim with the Sharks Without Being Eaten Alive,* said it very well when he stated: "Time is free, but it's priceless. You can't own it, but you can use it. You can't keep it, but you can spend it. Once you've lost it, you can never get it back." That is why I never take my time that I have been gifted from God for granted. I never undervalue the hours I have been gifted with to spend time with those I love and have the privilege to spend my time with.

When you give someone your time, you are giving them a piece of your life that you will never get back. Time, therefore, is a commodity that once spent, you will never gain back. So many people in this world have been ignorant towards the fact that the time you spend "living" is limited. You are not here forever, so why do so many of us expect someone else to be with us forever? Why do so many people take their most valuable commodity and toss it down the drain as though tomorrow is guaranteed? Why are so many people lacking powerful and loving relationships in their lives?

I believe there are many reasons behind this issue. However, the one very important reason so many people are not having deep connections with others and living their fullest life, is because they are not spending their time in the best way that they can.

If you want to deepen your relationship with yourself and with others, you must learn how to use the time that you were gifted with in a way that will enhance and empower your life and your relationships to a whole other level. A level where peace dwells deep within your soul. A level where joy shines through your eyes when you are with others. A level where love shines through your entire being, like the moon shines its light down on mother earth and lights up the entire night sky.

In order to deepen our relationships with ourselves and with others, we have to understand the difference between well-used quality time, and time that is just being used. It is very simple to understand if a person is just using their time, passing each day by like it never mattered, or is living a life where they realize that their time is their most valuable commodity, therefore, living each day to their fullest.

To understand if you are living a life where you are using your time well, I will give you a quick example that

can make you see if you or someone else is living their best life. Can you remember a time where you have run into a friend that you have not seen in quite some time, and asked, "Hey! How are you doing? What's been up? Anything new?" Then they respond with the phrase, "Oh, nothing much same things, different day."

I can't tell you how much I dislike hearing this phrase. I often hear it when I ask people how they have been and what have they been up to. It irks me to a level of complete frustration and annoyance. I just want to explain to them how valuable their time is and that they need to start living a life worth remembering.

Anyway, I remember saying that phrase a lot when growing up because I would hear my family say it every time we were out and about grocery shopping or at a family get together, or something in that nature.

Growing up, hearing those words as much as I did, caused me to say that phrase to others when I ran into them. And let me make this very clear to you–your word is the power that has been gifted to you directly from God, and you have the ability to create it however you want. Therefore, what you say, you become.

What you become and where you are at in your life and in your relationships, can be understood by how you are using your words. Your word is a powerful force of which you have the ability to use to create the events, the relationships and the life in which you want to live. So, as I went on expressing my words in that way, I noticed over time, how true that statement had become in my own life! This scared the pants off of me!

The words that we use to describe the life we live or the relationship we are in can either empower us or break us down. I know this to be true because the words I used each day ended up causing my relationships and my life to become inanimate.

Once I started to see that my life became the words I

spoke, I learned just how powerful my word truly is. Your words do truly shape and create your world, your relationships, and ultimately the life you live. Be sure to do yourself a favor and be on guard as well as be careful when you hear someone else answer the question you ask them by saying, "Oh, nothing much. Same thing, different day!" If you do hear one of your friends say this to you, do them a great favor and speak up! I advise you to speak up and try to figure out if that is the truth or not. Become curious and learn about them a little bit more to see if the time they are using is being used wisely. I advise that if you have time while you are with them, do a deep dive to learn more. If you don't have enough time, reach out to them via text message later that night, and help them understand that life is meant to be lived fully, loved, and appreciated often.

Think about it. What do you think their relationship is like with their girlfriend, boyfriend, family, friends, wife, husband or kids? Do you think that, if that is their response, that their relationship is one that is promising, powerful, exciting and loving? Or do you think it is one that is mediocre, breakable and not so exciting? I am sure that their lives and relationships could become much more profound, meaningful, and vibrant if you help them out by making them more aware of the words they use. There are a few things I want you to make sure you realize if you do use this phrase or something similar.

Number one: make sure you know your truth. If you find yourself saying to someone same thing, different day, make sure you know that what you said is not the truth, and that it isn't just another day. For if you don't readjust and explain to yourself why it isn't just another day, your life will just become another wasted day. Don't waste your days. Your time is your life, use it consciously. Like I said before, your word creates your reality, your life, and your relationships.

If you say it so that you don't have to talk to someone, you must make sure after you say it, that you take the time, energy, and effort to explain to yourself how it is not the truth. The last thing you want to do is show up in your life or your relationships and treat them in a way that makes your life or them feel like it is just another day. Make your life and your partner feel special, loved, and appreciated daily. Use your time wisely and upgrade the time you spend with them by creating powerful words, habits, and goals that will empower you to live your best life.

Number two: that phrase is so unrealistic that you have no purpose in even saying it. However, know that when you do say it or some other phrase or word over and over again, your subconscious mind doesn't know the difference between what is real and what is fake.

So, don't let it think for one moment that your life is dull and black and white. For your life is beautiful and wonderful, and you are alive. Open your eyes to find the beauty in all that is around you. Understand how beautiful and wonderful your life is because you are alive.

It is your job to find a response like I did when someone asks you that question. The phrase that I like to use when I run into someone and don't have the time to talk is, "I can't complain, I am alive, I am here, and I am grateful." Then you're off. Empower yourself and your mind to live a better quality of life and have a deeper relationship with others by taking back what is yours–your time and your word.

24

WAKE UP CALL

> "It doesn't matter how MUCH time you spend with them. What matters is HOW you spend your time that you have with them."

— TYLER JOE STRATTON

Now, how can you start living a better quality of life, with deeper relationships with those you care about, by using your time in a way that is being well-used?

When looking up the basic understanding of the term, 'quality time', the dictionary defines it as, "Time spent in giving another person one's undivided attention, in order to strengthen a relationship." When was the last time you were with the person you cared about the most and you didn't allow all of your daily distractions to interrupt your undivided attention off of them?

When was the last time you were with your boyfriend, girlfriend, mom, dad, wife or husband, and didn't check your phone? When was the last time you were with the person you cared about the most and didn't just watch Netflix? Many people nowadays have this idea and think that a relationship can be built through social media, or by spending time together just by watching Netflix.

However, let me tell you a little secret, Netflix and social media are wonderful, but in order for you to build a powerful and loving relationship with your special someone, it cannot be built upon Netflix or by having a phone attached to your hand. That is not how you should spend your quality time with your favorite people.

These two things can come in handy, but they distract you from the main reason you are in a relationship–which is to connect and be with them! The point of your relationship is to deepen your connection with one another so you feel the vitality and joy that relationships can offer you.

The purpose of your relationship with someone is to do what humans were supposed to do. That is to serve each other through love and create soul-awakening relationships that make us feel fulfilled, loved and whole so that we can help others accomplish the same thing. How can you learn how to deepen the quality of time spent with the people you care about the most? Let me take you through the thoughts that have helped me deepen each one of my relationships:

SET MEANINGFUL INTENTIONS

As soon as I walk out of the door to go spend time with anyone, I make it my duty to set a meaningful intention. For example, I want you to think of someone you love and hold dear to your heart. I want you to close your eyes and see that person's smile. I want you to keep your eyes closed and picture the two of you hitting it off, connecting deeply, and living fully present in the moment with each other. Feel the love between the two of you for just a few moments. Once you feel that love storm in to your entire being, I want you to then feel the thought of finding out that the person that you just thought of in your mind will be gone tomorrow morning when you wake up.

If you knew that the person would no longer be here tomorrow, how would you spend the next twenty-four hours with them? What would your intention be? Would it be to be more loving? Would it be to give them your full attention and time finally? What would your purpose be if today was their last day knowing that tomorrow would be too late?

Take some time to think about this. Ponder it and allow these thoughts to fill your entire being for just a few moments. I'm sorry for taking you down this path, but some of you need to wake up! Some of you need to realize the truth, which is that death is upon each one of us.

We must stop hiding and running away from this profound truth. For when we stop hiding and running away from the truth that our time and our loved one's time here on earth is not forever, we finally begin to realize just how precious our time and their time truly is.

This deep truth, if felt, will send you on the path toward living your best quality of life with other people. It sickens me to know how many of us hide the thought of death so well. Many of us either don't think about it at all or hate to think about it when we do. Instead of facing it and learning from it, many run from it. When we run away from death and don't hold it in our awareness, we run away from living intentionally, fully, deeply, and on purpose.

Not living on purpose will lead you to live a life that will cause you never to experience true fulfillment. You have a purpose here on earth and it's up to you to let the angel of death be your greatest teacher. Let the thought consume you for a little while. Play with it in a way that will help you understand that in order for you to advance the quality of your life and the quality of time that you spend in your relationship with others, you must act and show up the way you would if you found out that the person you loved had twenty-four hours to live.

LIVE INTENTIALLY! LIVE ON PURPOSE! LIVE LIKE IT WILL BE YOUR LAST DAY!

Everyone knows how they should show up when they are with someone who cares about them, so don't over complicate this, stress about this, or think for one moment you can't do it! You are God's highest form of creation, made from the highest of energy, love. That's right, and you were made out of love to give love to others.

This is what you were designed to do. Don't overthink it. Loving others will come naturally to many who spend some time with themselves and connect deeply with their heart. If you do find yourself unable to love yourself or others, here is a little bit of direction that will help you understand how you should show up.

First of all, you should show up ready to love, lead, and serve them in the best way that you can. With love in your heart! If you master this, the rest will fall into place naturally. You should respect them, listen to them, give them your undivided attention, be grateful that you are there with them, compliment them and make them feel like they are the only thing or person who matters in your life at that very moment.

The secret to enjoying those you are around is to be fully present with those you are with. Keep your attention on them and focus on nothing else besides making them feel heard and seen. Relationships are not hard if we keep it simple. However, many of us still find relationships some of the most challenging parts of our lives.

If you are someone who is experiencing a tough time in your relationships, it is probably because of the problem that we all face, including me. We all get lazy in our relationships. You see, when we are with those who want to spend their time with us, we go through the motions and don't put in the effort to generate a great and loving relationship with them. The lack of effort is the reason so many great relationships wither away.

Make it your life's mission and duty every time you walk out one door and through another, to give your full effort to live fully and be there for others. Being able to show up on purpose and being willing to provide them with your full effort, will increase the depth of the relationship you have with them. You will begin to feel the vibrancy and livelihood that relationships have to offer you.

The reason why I make it my mission and duty to show up with the intention of being fully present in each one of my relationships is because the feeling of regret is the one thing I fear the most. You see, I am not afraid to think about death or to die. I am not afraid to think about the fact that the ones I love are going to die. However, I am afraid of not have given that person who I spend my time with, the best of who I know I can be for them and everyone I interact with.

Not showing up as my best self and most loving self are the moments I find myself living in regret. I hate regretting anything in life! That is why when I think about the feeling of regret, I begin to transform into a greater version of myself. For when I think about regret, I will strive to live my life to its fullest potential. For I never want to find myself living a regretful life.

This truth helps me to show up in my relationships as more loving, more joyful, more open, more alive, and more present with each and every one of them who I spend my time with. Therefore, when that day with them comes to an end, I can look back and know I didn't regret the time I spent with those I care about.

Let morality teach you how to live. Let morality teach you how to love. Let morality teach you how to enjoy the relationships you are in. Stop running from your own death and the death of others. Walk into this thought with an openness and acceptance of the truth. For the truth will set you free, and it will free you up to live a life worth living. It will set your relationships on fire and it will set your soul on the run for a greater quality of life and a deeper connection to those around you.

When you run away from these thoughts and truths, your relationships with yourself and others become shallow and will break a lot easier. Don't regret the time you spend with others, for it's the only thing you will spend that you won't get back.

Your quality of time is based on how you use your time and how you feel while using it. So, the next time you are with someone who cares about you, I ask you kindly, to set the intention of being there with them, fully engaged, loving, joyful and peaceful, and realize that if you are not there with them entirely, you might as well not be with them at all.

Your time is the greatest gift you can give someone. Spending quality time with someone will genuinely help you build a deeper relationship with others, as well as increase your overall quality of life. As long as you continue to have time to live, you will always have time to strengthen your relationships with those who matter the most.

25

SEPARATING YOUR WORK FROM YOUR LIFE

<blockquote>

"Leave it all behind you. Don't let it define you. Your workday is just your workday, not your life."

— TYLER JOE STRATTON

</blockquote>

If you can learn to separate your work or school life from your actual life, you will always be ready to go home to your loved ones in a happy, healthy and positive state of mind. And when you are in this state of mind, your relationships will be happier, healthier and more positive. This type of mindset will lead to long-lasting and loving relationships. Makes enough sense, right? But yet, many men, women, boys and girls out there, still let their work life or school life be their actual life.

Whatever goes on at work or at school is what defines their mood, thoughts, feelings, their day, and even sometimes, their entire life. Don't let your work life become your actual life!

I give credit to my father for teaching me this powerful

lesson, without ever really sitting me down to actually teach it. You see, this lesson that he taught me, I learned when he would come home from work. I have learned a lot from both of my parents by watching closely, the things they did and didn't do. They taught me so much! However, I didn't grow up always having the perfect role models; I grew up having people I didn't always want to be like and seeing situations I never wanted to find myself in.

Not all of us are dealt the right cards, but that didn't stop me from reshuffling the hand I was dealt in hopes for a better outcome. You see, throughout my childhood years, I found myself observing my mom, my dad and my older brother's energy, mood and body language. For I knew what to expect from them based on these characteristics and the vibes they were giving off.

Being an introvert put me in a place where I loved to spend a lot of time alone. The more time I would spend alone, the more I become aware of just how sensitive I am when I am around other people. Being sensitive has its perks. One of the perks I have learned to use to benefit my life, is understanding how others are feeling based on the energy or vibe they would give off.

I've learned how to separate my thoughts and feelings from others, which really helps me to understand what it is that those around me are going through and what their day might have looked like. It is my sensitivity and my ability to deeply observe others that has helped me learn that in order to build a powerful and loving relationship with others, I must separate my work life from my home life.

Your home life is your actual life. This is the time that you are in your environment and you become the person you truly are when no one is watching. When I talk about your actual life, I mean the person you are outside of your job and all the worries, stress, and problems that are causing you to be a person who you don't like being. Therefore, your actual life is the person you are without the job, the worries, stresses and problems that come with it.

Being raised in a single parent household throughout most of my life, I have learned so much. One of the things I have learned was just how hard my father worked to support my brother and I. That man has taught me so much about love, life, and everything in between. He has taught me about leadership and the sacrifices a great and loving leader takes in order to get through life's most difficult times.

My father was the type of father who made sure that I was always okay mentally, physically and spiritually. He was the type of father who would eat last and make sure that my brother and I were taken care of before he was. He taught me about hard work and how to never give up, even when hard work became too hard.

My father has taught me about the importance of respecting others and the importance of love. My father has taught me so much about how to be a gentleman and how we should always trust and pray to God, for He is always here with us and supporting us. My father has taught me so much more, but the one thing that he has taught me without actually sitting me down and teaching me, was to make it your duty to do everything you can to separate your work life from your home life. In other words, make it your duty to keep the negative thoughts, worries, and events from work, at work. Never bring them home with you. For if you bring those thoughts, worries, emotions and events back home with you, your relationships with those in your home can be ruined.

Throughout the years of living with my hardworking and loving father, I noticed how sometimes the household energy would fluctuate day to day. You see, each day would bring two different vibes and it all was based on how my dad's workday went.

If the workday went well or even normal, when he got home, he would be full of light and love. The blinds would be open, the country music would be playing, and he would be preparing a home-cooked meal for my brother and I. However, on the days that his workday didn't go so well, meaning it was a bad day, the blinds in our house would be closed, the house would be dark, the television would be on, and we would be lucky if we spoke more than a few dozen sentences from the time he came home to the time he would say to both my brother and I, "Sweet dreams, say your prayers, and I love you."

Day in and day out, my father's mood, energy and mind would change, along with our home's energy, depending on how his day went at work. While these days seem to pass by slowly, looking back, the years seem to slip by so quickly. I came to realize, as the years went on, that my memories I hold close to my heart from those days, were the memories in which my father would leave his work life at work, and let his fatherly, loving spirit enter the home as he walked through the door.

Leaving your work life at work, will help you to enjoy a deeper connection with those whom you come home to or enjoy life with. It will help you to enjoy your down time after work just a little bit more. And the best part are the memories you will make that you will take with you to the grave, if you can separate your work life from your home life.

You see, the days my father walked into the house as the man whom he knew he truly was, are the days in which memories were created, and those are the memories that I will take to the grave with me. The memories that I have been blessed with, and that you can be blessed with as well, will all be created by leaving your work life at work.

The memories that I will hold on to are the times that my father separated his work life from his home life by being a loving father for his two boys once he walked through the door.

These memories originated from the times when I would come home after football practice. The windows and blinds would be open and fresh air filled the house. My dad would be preparing a home-cooked meal on the grill, welcoming me home with a warm calming smile, a hug that was filled with love, and a kiss on the head that would always remind me that I was blessed to have him as my father.

These are the memories I will share with anyone who asks about my father. For these are the memories that have helped build my loving and hope filled heart. These are the times that helped deepen my relationship with my father and make it one that is powerful and loving.

No matter where you are at in life, you have a job to do and to pursue. No matter the job you are in, whether it be a school student or a construction worker, learning to separate your work life from your actual life will be a powerful thing because you will be able to build powerful and loving relationships with those who matter the most to you.

By leaving work outside of your home, you will be able to spend your undivided attention on taking care of your kids or enjoying your family, that special person you love, or even yourself. By separating your work life from your actual life, you will be able to laugh a little bit harder at the dinner table or in the living room in front of the television, which was where we ate our meals.

You will be able to experience what it is like to enjoy living amongst others, and more importantly, you will get to enjoy life with those who care about you the most. You will be able to build a strong trust that will allow you all to communicate openly and truthfully, without feeling like what you have to talk about will cause a fight of some sort.

By leaving your work life at work and settling into your home life once you get home, you will build fun memories and powerful, loving and deep relationships that you can take with you to your grave.

I will end this section of the book with this: Don't let your work life be your whole life. Don't let your work define you if you don't like the work you do. You must separate the two by figuring out who you want to be before entering your home and how you want to show up before walking out of one door and through another.

Your life is going to end one day, as will your parents, grandparents, aunts, uncles, brothers, sisters, as well as your closest friends. All the people you care about will one day pass away. Don't allow another day be wasted away just because you are all caught up in your work life. Don't carry around that negative energy and ruin your relationships with those who you surround yourself with.

Make sure that if you want your life to be a memorable one where the relationships you have with others are powerful and loving, make sure that you do this one simple task at the end of the day within your journal or even in your phone:

Ask yourself, "Do I regret how I've treated the ones I love and care about today?" If that answer is yes, learn to understand and get a clear understanding of why you regret it. Was it how you spoke to them? Was it how you acted toward them? If the answer is yes, make sure that you set the intention of how you want to show up tomorrow.

Set the intention to be the person whom you want to become by saying who you will be tomorrow. Set the intention and be that person, for when you are living in congruence with that person you know you truly can be, it will help you to go to bed with a peace of mind knowing that you've respected, loved and enjoyed everyone who loves and cares about you. Never go to bed mad. Make sure you separate your work life from your actual life, if you want to have a powerful and loving relationship with those who are waiting for you to get home.

PART III

KEY #3: BUILDING A RELATIONSHIP WITH GOD

"Just as a relationship with your best friend would soon turn sour if you stopped speaking, so too will our relationship with God."

— MARGARET FEINBERG

God, if you are there, whoever you are, where ever you may be, hear me out. I can't do this on my own. I have tried, and I am failing. Everything that I have ever wanted in life and worked so hard for, cried for, bled for, sacrificed my time for, has been taken away from me.

I have tried to be strong, to show them that I am different, to prove to myself that I am strong enough to need no one's help, to show no weakness and to stand tall. To be a faithful man with a good heart.

God, I am breaking, and I can't do this on my own. I am sorry for all that I have done, and for all the times I have ignored and betrayed you and withheld my love from you. God, if you are there, if you can hear me, if you can feel me, I NEED YOU. I can't do this on my own, nor do I want to do this on my own any longer. I need you, like a heart needs a beat. I need you, like the sky needs the stars, to show the world, that in pure darkness, it is still beautiful. I need you, like infinity needs no end. I need you like the devil needs your soul. I need you like love needs trust. I need you like I can only hope you need me.

Oh my God, can you hear me, can you feel me? If you are there, I surrender. I want this pain to end. I want this depression to decay. I want these thoughts of suicide to be forgotten like tears in the rain. I want these feelings that are stripping my life away to get lost inside the depths of hell, to never return again. God, I ask that you help me receive my life back. God, I ask that you help me open my heart back up to a love that will shatter my heart wide open so I can feel fully alive again.

I want the feeling of joy, gratitude, love and appreciation, running through my entire being, through every vein and inside every cell of my body, my mind and my soul. So that my soul can awaken from the depths of hell that it has been living in for far too long.

I need your help to set my mind, my body and my soul free from all the pain and suffering. Help awaken my entire being and help me feel as though I am myself again, no longer lost in the wilderness of doubt, fear, depression, and misery.

I surrender to you, my, God. I need you like the world needs you, now more than ever before. Heal us. Love us. Fill our hearts with love, our minds with hope, and are souls with life. Teach us about who we are and how to be loving and kind people toward ourselves and others.

Help us to love ourselves more fully and to have a deeper appreciation for life. Help us to see the truth, there being nothing more beautiful, more perfect, more real, more vulnerable, more awe-inspiring than to see love in its purest and unforgettable form.

We all need you. Whoever you are, wherever you may be,

if you can hear me, if you can feel me, know that I am here waiting for you to return into my heart and craft me into the loving, kind, and helpful man you have always wanted me to be. Equip me with the inner strength and everlasting love to be of service to those who are in need.

For I am here for them. For those who cry the same cry, live the same pain, battle the same wars in their minds as I have, and lived in internal misery.

Help me be the man I must be to be there for those who are lost and in need of help to make their way out of the wilderness of brokenness and back to their homes and become in-tune with their hearts again.

My God, help me accept your divine love and soften my heart so I can fulfill my mission, which is to help others build powerful and loving relationships that will withstand a lifetime of struggle. Help me help them. I am here to love, lead and serve them into a happier, healthier, more positive and fulfilling life.

Open my fear-filled heart, take my hand, and guide me, for I surrender my heart to love, so that I can help those who are like me as well as myself, be the best that we can be for each other and all of humanity. For I have felt you in my heart before and I have heard the voice of God speak to my soul that night as I laid in bed before I fell asleep.

I felt your presence, and heard you speak to my heart, and tell me that it was my mission to help others create a meaningful life that they will love. So they can learn how to use that knowledge to make an impact and a difference in the lives of others.

Help me to love them, to lead them, and to serve them, with a loving and open heart, mind, and soul. God, if you are there, hear my hearts cry, for I need you.

That was the message I cried out to God, who I had lost my connection and my relationship with growing up through some of the roughest years of my life. Not having a good relationship with God throughout many years of my life, never really bothered me until my breaking point.

I mean, I had heard of God, but never took time out of my day to build a relationship with God throughout my years of growing into a man. I never truly understood the point of praying, connecting and building a relationship with God, when all of my life had been a constant battle and war with myself, others and even with God.

Constantly fighting my inner and outer world battle left me to think if there was a God, I wouldn't be in so much misery. Therefore, I never truly saw the point in going to any church, for all I ever felt when I tried to go to a church was judgement from those sitting around me. I often found myself in a great amount of confusion listening to the men and women at the front. Worst of all, I walked out feeling even more beat up and less accepted than when I first walked in.

I thought the church was a place that any man, woman or child, no matter what age, could enter and connect with God, feel the love from God, learn about God, and be accepted by those in the church.

Now I am not saying that church is not a place people should go to. I know church, for some of my friends and people I know, is the only place they feel love, peace, joy, and God. However, I want to make myself clear and explain that what I am doing here is sharing my experience in the churches that I have gone to as a guest. I've observed the teachings, lessons, and feelings I get when I tried to build my relationship with God.

Maybe I haven't found the church, or perhaps I haven't explored long enough. Either way, the church wasn't where I developed my meaningful relationship with God, and I want you to know that is okay with me.

Before discovering how I would build my relationship with God, the relationship I have had was one that was so very distant. It was so distant that a rocket to the moon still couldn't connect us. As I tried to find myself and connect to

God, I found myself somewhat frustrated as time went on, and nothing seemed to work or make me feel closer to God.

I couldn't blame God for our distant relationship; I had so much destructive hate and hurt in my heart, that I didn't want to be around me either. If I didn't want to be with me, and others didn't want to be around me, then why on earth would some God who created the heaven and the Earth, man and woman, so perfect and so pure, want to be connected and close to me?

You see, I tried to build that relationship by searching to find THE church; I tried to find where I felt accepted and loved, and where I could connect to that greater divine source from above. I searched and searched until I just gave up. My conclusion after the search was that I didn't need God. Nope. I could do this on my own. I will forget God like I thought God had forgotten me. I will ignore God like God ignored my young broken heart that became filled with pain and misery.

I mean, you can't know what you're missing if you've never had it, right? I thought, "I don't know God, and therefore, I don't need God." So, throughout my childhood and teenage years, I continued to ignore God, like you try to ignore your ex on social media. I ignored God like a drunk ignores their pain by slamming down another bottle of beer. I ignored God like a liar ignores the truth.

As my stubborn self continued on, everything I loved, like my family, dreams and my football career, drifted away as if they never even existed or ever even mattered. This ultimately caused my gentle heart to feel the same pain and misery that I could never run far enough from.

Have you ever experienced something like this? Have you ever experienced a time in your life where the things you seem to love the most, hurt you the most because of the separation that would take place between you and them, or you and it?

What I have learned through my break ups and separations, is that it is the separation from two into one that will break the hearts of many. After many years of casting myself away and separating myself from God, I began to discover a lot of things about God while being separated from Him.

What I have learned, as the years went on, was the more I separated from God, the more He grew closer to me and me to Him. I was just unaware. And it was only at the moment when I stepped back to reflect on my life that I saw just how closely God has been working in my life.

It helped me to realize that everything in my life that has happened to me, has actually happened for a reason greater than the problem that I was facing. All thanks to God!

While feeling lost, depressed, angry and distant from God, I discovered that we are all here for a very special purpose. While uncovering our purpose we will begin to create our own life story that will have God hidden in every chapter of our story. While we all adventure off into life and the great unknown, we all will write our life story daily and we will survive every storm we face because God is there in the storm with us. Crazy, right?

No matter how far we travel from God or what storm we face, He is there with you at all times. To really know and feel this, you must become silent and feel His presence by taking a step back from everything that is going on. Become fully present, fully engaged, fully accepting and fully appreciative of the moment you are in.

As you step back and become fully engaged in life's current moment, there is where you will find that the great God almighty and love is there with you, every step of the way.

As each one of us begins to build our relationship with God, we will soon discover more love and light in our life. Not just any love and light, but the love and light from the highest God.

If you know you need more love, joy, truth, happiness, and light in your life, then let me help you see that the way to having it all is by allowing God in your life by becoming more sensitive and silent in the moment. Submerge yourself in total solitude. Because it is in solitude where I have found my answers to all my problems and where I have found my loving God.

This is the final step to living your fullest quality of life! You see, in my eyes, everyone wants to be cared for and, more importantly, loved deeply and meaningfully. If you are like me, or anyone else who holds this truth close to their heart, then you must understand that God is love.

This truth was something I discovered while feeling distant from God. You see, while feeling distant from God, I didn't feel deeply connected to true everlasting love. I only found this to be true when I began to build a great relationship with God and noticed the love, joy, peace, and happiness that started to settle in my heart.

Sometimes you need to distance yourself and create alone time, so you can connect with who you are, and discover for yourself who and what God truly is. While on this journey of separating myself from God to find out who God is, I made a few discoveries that have helped me build a powerful and loving relationship with God.

I hope to supply you with exceptional and helpful information that will hopefully help you do the same! But before I go ahead and give you the powerful discoveries that have helped me build an excellent relationship with God, let me explain to you why everyone should build this relationship with God!

26

WHY BUILD A RELATIONSHIP WITH GOD

" "God is love, and all who live in love, live in God, and God lives in them."

— 1 JOHN 4:16

Your relationship with God is one of the most unique, powerful and life-changing relationships you will ever have in your life. It is the one relationship that will always be there with you and for you, even in the times you are not there for yourself.

God is there even when you have lost yourself along the way to getting to where you want to go. If you truly want to live your fullest life and soar to your ultimate human heights, you will let God in by letting go daily.

For a life with God, is a life where you can stand confidently, courageously, and joyfully open before the world! It's a life in which I strive to live daily. A life full of confidence, courage, and joy!

A life with God will allow you to give your truest and

fullest heart without the fear of getting hurt. For you know that you are always supported and the greatest of all Gods has your back and your heart. A life with God is a life where we get to live in our finest and highest state of being. It is a state where we get to receive, give and live in joy, truth and love. Love is the greatest of all reasons why everyone should begin to build a meaningful relationship with God.

God is the definition of love and is the one responsible for the everlasting love that flows through everyone and everything. Building a loving relationship with God is something everyone should really begin to consider. For God is what created all of us and where we all started, and where we will one day return.

You see, our spirit was created by the loving hands of God. We were made from love, meant to love and feel everlasting love. When we start to build a relationship with God and learn to let go and let love in to our hearts, we will notice that life will start to feel more alive, more purposeful and joyful!

For example, do you remember the first time you ever let go and fell in love with someone? Do you remember during that time, experiencing what many call puppy love, where you and your significant other couldn't seem to get enough of one another? Where everything you two did together was full of excitement, hugs, kisses, laughs, and nothing seemed to ever get in the way of the love you had for each other?

Can you remember how excited you were when you two fell in love and got to hang out with each other after your classes or sometime after work? Courageously open your heart and think back to the time when you first fell in love. How would you explain how you felt during those times you were in deep love? How was life during those times? Was it full of aliveness, joy, excitement and love or was it still dull, closed off, and unfulfilling?

I bet it was anything but dull, closed off, and unfulfilling. I bet you two felt the magical energy of love enter and flow through your entire being which allowed you both to see the beauty of life and just how special life was and how great love truly is. I bet you felt like you finally had a higher purpose for your life, and you knew what you were here to do during that time.

I know I felt that magical sensation and so much more, anytime I would allow myself to become more vulnerable and open my heart back up. Letting go and letting God in has allowed me to open my heart up again to the love my soul craved for a very long time. Opening my heart has helped me realize just how much I was missing out on in my life and how much better my life could become with love in my life.

However, when it comes to relationships with other humans, what seems to happen to these first-time puppy love relationships, is that in time, they begin to slowly separate from one another. I am not saying they all do; I am just saying that many of them end up being a lesson rather than anything more.

As time passes by, the two of you begin to lose the connection you once had ever so slowly. As this connection starts to become as lost as your cell phone service becomes lost in the wilderness, something happens to love. It seems to me that the moment the connection to our significant other begins to lose its reception, love begins to die, and so does our vibrancy toward everyday life. But it doesn't have to be like that.

You don't have to lose love just because you are lost or are missing that once-powerful connection with your significant other. And more importantly, you don't have to begin to forget who you know you are and can be. Your joy, love, and excitement toward life can continue, even if that one relationship with your significant other does not.

You truly have the power not to allow yourself to lose yourself and end up feeling everything but positive, loved, and full of life, like you once did. There is always going to be a way to explore the love your heart is seeking, even when you have no one else to love.

God is the way to everlasting love, joy, excitement, and fulfillment that your heart seeks for. Especially in the moments when all you can see is the darkness and the lack of love you are facing. There is no better time than right now to begin to work on your relationship with your God.

What I learned in my life is that it was through the times of chaos and heartbreak when my connection and relationship with God began to take place. In those darkened times of chaos and heartbreak, you need God's love more than ever. So, when you recognize confusion, heartbreak, or struggle in your life, do yourself a big favor and begin the building process the right way by becoming a little bit more courageous.

Begin to build and focus on the relationship that means the most—your relationship with God. The truth is, your relationship with God is the relationship that you have been trying to create and find within other human beings. It is the relationship that you have been searching for within others. Know this and look no further.

The relationship and love that you have been searching for in others are found within the relationship between you and God. The most important relationship your heart is seeking to find, is a relationship with God. Whether you were born to believe this or not. Your heart has been seeking out an everlasting and unbreakable relationship with God, not with others. It is the relationship with God that will finally set you free, make your heart feel more whole than ever before.

In this world, many have distended away from God and have been confused for quite some time, questioning their belief, faith and religion. But let me assure you that the equation which you have been trying to solve in order for you to feel fulfilled, loved, healed, wanted, needed and so much more, will become solved once you realize it's a relationship with God that you have been trying to create within other people that will unlock your heart to experience a greater quality of life. This is the relationship that will set you free and create a life full of love and joy! Let the building begin.

27

UNDERSTANDING WHO AND WHAT GOD IS

" "Love to me, is Godly, and God to me, is Love. And that is why Love is Everything."

— TYLER JOE STRATTON

In order to build a powerful and loving relationship with God, you must understand who and what God is. You see, many people throughout life have a hard time understanding who God is, as well as understanding how to build a relationship with God because they've never understood who God was to them.

Many people can't relate to God, and therefore, there seems to be a disconnection between them and God. Tell me; how hard is it for you to build a powerful and loving relationship with someone who you can't relate to? I find it pretty hard. Heck, sometimes I find it hard to build a connection and loving relationship with someone who I can relate to.

However, when it comes to building a relationship with God, there is always one thing that will help you relate to

God, as well as learn who God is to you. That one thing is called LOVE.

In the very moments you find yourself feeling that powerful feeling of love run through your entire being, is the moment you have touched the surface of your highest self and have connected deeply to God. Can you remember a time when you have reached a state of living in your highest self? Where love led the way?

I know throughout my life, there have been multiple times where I have reached my highest self and have felt the presence of God awaken my entire being. Every year, right around the month of December, my connection with God seems to enhance naturally and becomes stronger.

Being raised as a Christian, my family celebrates many of the Christian holidays. Especially Christmas. As the days pass by and the twenty-five-day countdown until Christmas comes on the television, playing my favorite holiday season shows and movies, my spirit becomes more and more in touch with God.

As the days grow closer to December 25th, my excitement towards life increases, as does my love for family, friends, myself, and God. As a child, can you remember the night before Christmas in your household? Can you remember the emotions you were feeling and experiencing? I bet that you can remember a time where you had more energy and love in your heart the night of Christmas Eve, that you found it hard to calm down, and even harder to fall asleep.

The excitement and love that was running through your entire being; that was God. God was with you and you can always tap into that energy anytime that you want, for God is always with you. You just have to be willing to open yourself up and allow that feeling back in to your life.

I know that I have also experienced my highest self and have felt the presence of God awaken my entire being during times right around my birthday. I am sure I will experience the same thing the day I become a married man.

There are times in life that God will present Himself to you, and these are just a few times of which I know that my connection and relationship with God has become more real and more relatable. The times in your life that you have experienced love, are the times which you have experienced God. God is love. To understand God is to understand love.

In order to build a powerful and loving relationship with God so you can start to live your fullest life, feel enriched with life, and always loved, you must understand a four-letter word that is overused and has seemed to have lost its divine trueness and power.

You must understand what love truly is. When you do, you will understand God and will then be able to build a powerful and loving relationship that will become more relatable.

Love is our beginning; it is where we were first started, and it is our final destination. Love is a divine energy, that when experienced, can give life a newer feeling that brings more magic, life and meaning into our lives. Love shouldn't ever be exhausting. It shouldn't leave you feeling stressed out, worried, less than, or unappreciated.

Love won't leave you feeling drained, it won't leave you depressed, lost, or distraught. Love just won't leave you, period. However, love is free, natural, and is a healer. Love is a friend and a protector. Love will never break you; it will build you and it will then help bring out the best in you.

Just like God does when you let Him enter your heart and bring Him back into your awareness. Building a positive relationship with love at the forefront will help us become those who set the stage for the future. We become the reason others believe in the goodness of people.

When you let love in, what you are truly doing is allowing God to be in your life. When you let it in, you will notice the magnificent feelings of love, compassion, generosity, kindness, empathy and forgiveness enter your life and become a part of who you were always meant to be.

However, in order to let love in and to truly allow God to be in your life so that you can build that everlasting relationship your heart is truly after, you must overcome this false disempowering belief. Which is the idea that there is not enough love in this world to give or receive. This is a false belief that will only destroy your relationship and connection with love.

Let me make one thing very certain about love. Love cannot be destroyed by any human. The truth about love that you must understand and learn to accept with an open heart is that love just like God is a divine and powerful energy that is always flowing, present and accessible.

To know God, you must know love. To know love is to know God. We must let go of the limiting belief that love is something that comes and goes when the person who we love comes and goes. Love is always accessible and abundant in everyone's life. It isn't something that can be taken from you.

The truth is that it is a powerful energy, just like God, that runs through you and allows you to experience the fullness of life so that you can reach your highest level of love, and lead and serve at levels beyond your wildest imagination.

The relationship you are after has always been one that is well-equipped with love and life. God is just that relationship. Our relationship with God is one that will release the truest, deepest and purest love of all. And it is our upmost desire to be in a relationship where we can love others and be loved by others.

That is why when we get to experience love and what it is like to be loved, it becomes our most enlivening energy that drives us to reach every goal, offer a loving hand, and enable us to help others live a life worth remembering.

Surely, we would all like to have more love in our lives, and with God, that is possible. For God is love, and love is God. Opening yourself up to love is one of life's greatest secret treasures that can be discovered and unlocked once we make love and God our primary focus.

Building this relationship will help you to feel more connected, present, caring, and empathetic, and your ability to influence this world will become easier than ever. Love is the Divine tool given to us from God.

Once we learn to understand how to become open to it in our lives, we will become more open to God and those around us. That is when this divine tool given to us from God can help us create a life where we can love ourselves deeper, build powerful and positive relationships that will deeply fulfill our emotional and social life, as well as live the fullest live we were meant to live.

28

THE WORST PRISON

 "The worst prison would be a closed heart."

— POPE JOHN PAUL II

W hen you consciously decide to close up your heart, deny love or run away from love, it will affect every cell in your body, mind, and soul. Simply because love is the very source of who we are and who God created us to be. To feel love, is to feel God and to feel God, we must be courageous enough to keep our hearts open so that we stay connected and close to God. For the worst prison one will ever experience in his or her life is a life where their heart is closed off.

Denying love is the ultimate crime one can commit in their life and it is the main way we destroy our relationship with The Big Three. Closing our hearts and denying love to enter in to our being will only raise havoc in our hearts, chaos in our souls and misery in our minds. In essence, when we deny love, we deny who we are and who God is.

When we deny love, we will soon find ourselves locked

inside a prison cell where the bars are made only out of our fears. You see, denying love has been something I have done many times throughout my life. Oftentimes, I would find myself running away from love every time it was near. Which ultimately left me trapped inside a prison that I created. Within this prison, where no love resides, the world seemingly loses its hope filled color it once had and everything that once was beautiful begins to turn gray.

As life continues on behind the bars created by fear, life, in general, seems to have little to no meaning. You begin to feel lifeless and hopeless. You begin to lose your spiritual fulfillment that was once all around you and within you. At that moment when I no longer feel God in my life, is the moment I find myself lost, alone and as empty as a broken smile.

Before you can begin to live your fullest life and step into a closer relationship with God, you must make it your aim and your highest intention to also understand how the closing of your heart is a harmful and painful way to live.

A closed off heart will lessen the strength of the connection between you and your God. When you find your heart closed up from the past pains of being judged, rejected, crushed, embarrassed, hurt, or broken, the connection between you and God is weakened.

Closing up your heart closes down the bridge that will connect you to God. And yet, so many people still live their lives with the absence of love in their hearts just because they believe love was what got hurt or broken by another.

However, let me remind you that it wasn't your heart or love that was lost or broken, it was your ego that was hurt and broken. Love itself has no enemies and can never be hurt. But because so many never learn that truth, they never truly get to build a loving and powerful connection with God.

Have you ever been hurt, or lost someone you truly loved? If you have, then you know just how tough it is to get through those times. For it is in those times, that many have closed up their heart and decided to build a shield around it so they could block out the one thing the shield was built to protect; love.

Building a shield around your heart won't stop you from getting hurt. It will only lessen the feeling of love and weaken the connection between you and God, who you need more than ever. So, make sure that when pain enters into your life, you remain open to love and not beat yourself up and close yourself off to it, for it will only cause you more suffering if you decide to guard your heart.

It is the common belief and idea that many still live by, that when you get hurt by someone you love, you must "protect your heart" from others. The moment you believe this to be true is the moment you begin to believe the false reality that love itself has enemies, that people are trying to shoot down every time love showed itself to you.

Love never takes the hit when the shots of hate and brokenness are fired into your life. Love is forever flowing and always present. Love is God and is there to help and always be there for you. Love is an energy that is never absent from your life.

The truth is, that when the shots of hate and brokenness impel your being, it was your ego that took the hit, not love. Love has nothing to do with hurt, pain, suffering or brokenness. Love is the opposite of the hurt, pain, suffering, and brokenness. Love is unaffected by misery and will never be here one moment and gone the next. Just like God. So, if everything I am saying is true, then what happens to love when you are in a relationship with someone and they leave you and you no longer feel that love you once felt?

Love itself doesn't leave you. However, what leaves is your awareness of love and God's presence within your life. You see, the only thing that is absent from your life when you believe love is what is absent from your life is your awareness of love. In other words, you have taken your focus off the feeling of love that has made you feel empty.

When you feel love, and have love in your life, it is because you've allowed yourself to focus on love and have allowed your heart to be open and accept God into your life because you wanted to. When you have "lost" love, all you did was take your attention away from feeling love and put your attention on the shield that will protect you from feeling love.

To understand God, you must understand love. God's love is infinite, and it isn't something that anyone can own or can lose at any given time. It is not something that is becoming extinct and scarce. Love is not delicate. It is stronger than any amount of steel. It is unbreakable, just like your God.

God will take away your pain and suffering once you allow yourself to focus on it once more. For love is divine, and it is a spiritual energy that was created by God to help you understand Him.

God and His love are at this very moment, flowing through the entire universe, throughout every plant and animal. Love is truly the greatest way to connect and understand God. Just like God Himself, love is flowing through every one of your enemies, your family members and the 7.6 billion people who still remain on this earth today.

Do you not see the truth that love is God, and God is love? And the way to connect with God is to keep your awareness focused on love and to keep your heart open to love? Love, just as God does, exists everywhere and within everyone! So very freely it runs through everyone, abundantly giving in everyday life, and never giving up on you or anyone else.

Just as God has never been absent from your life! He has always been with you and continues to be with you every step of the way.

So, I ask you to not let your awareness of God's love diminish from your life even when you get hurt and want to believe you have lost love. Always remind yourself that your connection with your God can be found when you allow love to enter your heart.

Let no amount of hurt, pain, sadness, misery or brokenness tear you away from love, for it was never love that got hurt, it was just your ego. I know what I say isn't easy to do, especially when you are feeling betrayed and miserable. But I do know that it is you who has allowed love in and to be felt. And it is you who is not allowing love into your life and allowing your pain and suffering to replace the love that you were once aware of.

It is you who has the capability of creating a new vision during the times of doubt, and it is you who can make a new choice, one where you can either live with God in love or dive into the depths of hell with the devil.

Don't let the pain of yesterday follow you into your day today, causing your walls of "protection" to come up and guard your heart. Don't let your pains of yesterday ruin your connection with God today. Live in today and let go of yesterday's pain.

Make it your duty to go into the new day with an open heart so that you can feel the presence of God in your life. If you can let go of the suffering and allow your heart to open, you will find that your connection with your God will become more powerful and loving than ever before.

Allow yourself to witness the truth as I have. Let yourself realize and accept that the walls of protection guarding your heart are only causing you to suffer more. For it is keeping out love, and it is keeping God out of your life. Don't allow yourself to shield God's presence because you won't allow love to flow freely and abundantly in your life, just because you were hurt.

The only way to stop the pain, suffering and heartache, is through love. Love is the answer, and God has more love for you than anyone else will ever have for you.

God's love is a real energy that can be felt anytime you want to feel it. It is divine, forever present, and always flowing through us and around us abundantly. The truth is, there is never a moment in your life where God, or His divine love, is not there for you to give to others and to receive for yourself.

To once again open yourself up to the relationship you have with God, you must also open yourself back up to His love. For love is directly from God, and that is where you must begin to build your relationship with Him.

In order to build a relationship with God, you must open yourself to love once again. You must let go of the belief that love has enemies and that love can be taken away from you.

Make it your duty today, to begin to bandage up the wounds of the past and cast them into the heavenly sky of love. Let no amount of pain, suffering or false beliefs remain in the place where love should be. Make it your mission to be a light of shining love that will forever exist abundantly in the world in which you live.

Be amongst the few who build an everlasting relationship with their God by being so brave as to open up their heart to love once more. Choose to live a life that is walked with love every day.

For when you learn to let go of the pain and allow love to flow through you, your connection and relationship with God will become one that will help you live your fullest life. Now it's your time to not be afraid of the truth, that love is here to heal you, not hurt you. It is time you turn back to love.

29

COMMUNICATION IS KEY

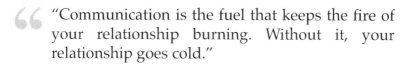 "Communication is the fuel that keeps the fire of your relationship burning. Without it, your relationship goes cold."

— WILLIAM PAISLEY

I'm sure she understood what I meant. It should have been obvious how I felt. It took me a very long time to learn that the most common source of miscommunication when it comes to any relationship is a very simple one: We routinely fail to realize just how little we are actually communicating. We seem to think we say a lot more than we actually do.

Throughout my past relationships there have been many times I believed that my behavior was much more expressive than it actually was. For instance, I often believed that my significant other, family member or friends could tell when something was wrong by how I presented myself. However, this is rarely the case because they rarely picked up on my signals and didn't have any idea what was going on inside my mind or what my problem was.

Miscommunication is detrimental in any relationship you have. Where there is no communication, there is no connection, and where there is no connection, there is no relationship.

This is one of the most important lessons I have learned after going through many failed relationships. When I say failed relationships, I just mean a relationship that didn't last as long as I thought it would have lasted.

My relationship with God is sort of like riding on a roller coaster. Sometimes it seems that I am on fire for God, and other times I don't feel a thing.

THE IMPORTANCE OF COMMUNICATION

When has communication not been one of the main keys that you've allowed to help you to unlock a great relationship? Communication is an important aspect in every healthy relationship, including your relationship with God.

The more time you spend with God and communicate clearly and honestly with an open heart, the deeper and more powerful your relationship with God will become.

As your relationship with God deepens through your communication, the more you will get to know Him and His love for you. As your relationship with God deepens through the way you enjoy communicating to Him, you will start to feel His love enter into your life, and your burdens, stresses, worries, illnesses, and heartbreaks won't feel so heavy.

It is always a great feeling to be able to turn to someone in a time of need but it's even better when you can turn to someone you can trust, count on, and who is also a good listener. Never being heard and holding in your negative thoughts and painful emotions, will cause you to suffer deeply and live a low quality of life. It might even cause you to disconnect from love and God.

I know in my life this has been the case many times. What I have learned throughout my life is you should never hold a negative thought or conversation in for too long. You need to effectively communicate your issues out of you in some way, shape, or form. You can express your concerns in many different ways. Some of the most popular and helpful ways that I enjoy releasing the negative thoughts, emotions, and conversations are either by writing in a journal, talking to a good friend or my favorite one, by talking to God.

If you find yourself in turmoil, stressed, overwhelmed, or feeling disconnected from yourself, others, or God, it is time that you let it go and have that conversation with God!

Human beings are relational. We were created in God's image and are known to be God's highest form and greatest creation. Our Father desires a personal relationship with us. He craves it as much as we crave it. He is aware, present, and compassionately involved in every detail of who we are and who we can become.

God does not require us to grow into a different version of ourselves in order to have a powerful and loving relationship or conversation with Him. For God is here now and has always been here with us.

He hears us when we speak to Him and he faithfully holds to His promise to be close to the brokenhearted and to love us unfailingly. God desires our communication with Him. He desires that we ignite a conversation with Him through prayer, so that is what we must learn how to do.

Learning to communicate effectively can sometimes be rather difficult. Sometimes you can't get your story across in a clear way. Sometimes you don't know what to say or how to say it. And sometimes it can feel as if no one is listening. Having a conversation can be frustrating at times which is why many would rather not have a conversation at all and just run away from them.

However, no matter how far away you try to run, you will always find yourself back in a conversation with yourself,

with others, or with God. That is why it is important to just
have the conversation as soon as you can. Learning to accept
and love myself a little bit more has helped me to hold the
conversations I need to have with God.

Now I love being able to turn to the ones I love and trust
in order to express what it is I am going through, but I find it
can be rather tough. There are times that I do find myself
expressing my truth, my thoughts, and emotions to those I
love which brings me a much-needed peace into my life.

To be able to vent and communicate my struggles,
stresses, and worries to those who love me, helps me feel
freer from all the negativity. It helps me to move on and not
feel so suffocated by the pain in which I am holding in.
However, when you don't have that loved one or best friend
to talk to, life can seem overwhelming and empty.

It can feel as though you are suffering and living with a
fake happiness. Faking your happiness will lead you down
the road of confusion, emptiness, and depression. That is why
it is important once you need to truly open up and talk to
someone, you talk to God first.

For your communication with God will do the same
things for you as a friend will, but what you will find is that
He is an even better listener and caretaker. And the best thing
about God is that He is always there for you, ready to listen
to you and love you powerfully and deeply.

He will always pick up the phone when you call him and
answer your questions when you ask them. You just have to
believe and have the faith that God is there with you as much
as you are there with yourself.

You are a beloved individual and have always been loved
by God, even when you didn't love Him or want a
relationship with Him. And because God has so much love
for you, He is willing to listen to you and hear your cries, feel
your pains, and be there to catch you when you fall.

Sometimes the reason why you fall is so you can feel the
presence of God in your life when He catches you. So, don't

be afraid of the fall. Too many times we want to zip through the valleys of life and to only dwell upon the mountain tops. However, the truth is, without the valleys there would be no such things as the beautiful mountain tops.

For there to be mountain tops, there need to be valleys. Also, for us to grow closer to God, we shouldn't blame God for every time it rains in our life. Because without the rain, nothing can grow. Without the storms, we wouldn't know what peace truly is. So, always be reminded of this truth in your mind and engraved in your heart.

He is near, and you can trust that He is Good, and He is your Father who is here to support you. So, the next time you find yourself in the middle of the wilderness feeling empty, alone, frustrated, and depressed, instead of praying to God asking Him to take you out of the wilderness, you should pray that He will teach you while in the wilderness.

Becoming more open and consistent with communicating with God will help you feel as though you are never alone, even when the going gets tough, and you find yourself in the valleys.

HOW TO COMMUNICATE

So how does one deeply communicate with God in order for them to not only build a powerful and loving relationship with Him but begin to feel His presence? How does one build a relationship where there is transparency, truth, and trust; a relationship where you can be open to everything and find peace at the end of the conversation.

That relationship is your relationship with God, and it can be built by communicating with God through many different types and methods. However, what seemed to help me communicate more clearly and feel God's presence when I would speak to Him through prayer is the following acronym called A.C.T.S: which stands for Adoration, Confession, Thanksgiving, and Supplication.

We are starting with adoration. Talked about early in my book, adoration sets your heart right. Giving praise to God for who and what He is, will help you to feel sincere gratitude for his love, kindness, and support.

Next is confession. Now confessions will help you to express what you are struggling with and help you clear some of the much-needed thoughts and problems you might be facing.

Then we have thanksgiving. Thanksgiving will help to open up your heart and move it toward a state of gratefulness.

And lastly, supplication. Supplication represents our prayer requests for the help, healing, blessing, beyond in which our hearts may be seeking.

Prayer is an opportunity to spend time with God. To really understand the heart of your Father, you need to pray or have a conversation with him. Just like you would with anyone else. In John 15:15, Jesus says, "He no longer calls us his servants, but calls us His friends." Talking with God truly does develop a deeper and more meaningful relationship with Him. That is why prayer is an essential tool that can enhance your communication with God.

Through prayer, you can manifest your relationship and dependence with God into existence. Prayer is far from being just merely a religious ritual. It is a spiritual practice that will also deepen your connection between you and your creator, just like love will deepen the connection between the two of you.

Prayer is one of the most important things you can do in order to strengthen the connection between you and God. It is a mighty tool that can release God's divine and loving power, in accordance with His will. It can bring about many amazing wonders and gifts, such as answers, healing, comfort, peace of mind, guidance, miracles and love.

In the Bible, Jesus said, "Whatever things you ask when you pray, believe that you receive them, and you will have them." (Mark 11:24) This, to me, is proof that God seeks to communicate with you and wants to communicate with you. For whatever you ask, your God is listening.

Now it is your turn to believe, with an open and trusting heart, that what you ask for will be received. God, like you, has desires. And it is His desire to be in a deep and close relationship with you. It is His desire to be in a close, present relationship with you and offer you guidance, encouragement, motivation, inspiration, truth, instruction and love. All so that you can fulfill your purpose and be the light and love that this world so truly needs.

If you start to open your heart up to love and communicate to God through prayer, you will hear Him speak, you will feel Him, and you will make it through the break ups, pain, and suffering. For He communicates to the heart of each and every individual who seeks Him. That is why you must open up your heart to love and let love in. For when you let love into your heart, God will communicate with you and you will become the person you were always meant to be.

Open yourself up to love and you will open yourself up to a deep communication that will lead you to a powerful relationship with God. Talking with God doesn't have to be complicated, so don't scare yourself off, for it isn't hard to do. It is actually one of the easiest conversations you will ever have. It is also one of the truest conversations you will ever have.

These conversations with God are like the 3 a.m. conversations that you have with your best friend. It is a conversation that is real, open, and vulnerable. Vulnerability creates connection, and connection creates love. Love is truth. And vulnerability is about sharing the truth you have in your heart with God.

Think about it for a moment. Your best friend is your best friend because they know all your deep secrets that you do not share with other people. They know your truth because you speak your truth with them when you can. That's why there's a feeling of freedom in the air when you are with them. And if you are seeking the same type of loving connection, you have with your best friend but with God, you need to own up to your truth and begin to voice your truth and desires to God.

We all want someone to love us for who we truly are, and God can be that person if you are ready to face your truths with Him and be real. So, don't be afraid to give it a try, and never think that you are doing it wrong. Just be open to communicating from your heart and letting your heart do the talking.

30

TALK TO GOD LIKE YOU TALK TO A FRIEND

" "Talking to God is like talking to our best friend on the phone. We may not see Him, but we know He is listening to our every word."

— TYLER JOE STRATTON

Communicating with God is like talking to a friend. When we find ourselves in a conversation with a friend or family member, many of us follow some type of general and basic format that will get the conversation started.

Think about the time you were at the store and you bumped into one of your friends or family members you hadn't seen in a while. You would normally start off by greeting them, by saying hello and asking them about themselves. As the conversation continued, you asked about their family, their health, their job, and if you were kind enough, you would have asked them about their wants and their needs, just to see if you could offer any advice or help.

As you asked them questions, there would always be a

middle part of conversation in between the question and the answer. The moment in between the question and the answer may have happened quickly or may have been several seconds long. However, during this moment in between the question and the answer, something subtle yet powerful happened.

This is where we took a moment to pause and listen to what they have to share with us. This is when we became actively engaged with them by being present with them and waiting for their answer. As we waited patiently and got the answer, we began to wrap up the conversation by bidding them fair well.

We did this to show them that we are genuinely interested in their well-being. And that's basically what God wants us to do when we pray to Him and have a conversation with Him.

We should respectfully and openly greet Him in prayer, ask Him questions and give Him thanks for the things that we are grateful for.

Your prayer may sound something like this: God, I am thankful that you have given me another day to live, to love, to lead and to serve. I am thankful that you are here with me, even when I ignore you and don't put you first. God, I am so very grateful that you are here to support me even when I don't support myself. I am so very grateful for the people in my life and those you have taken out of my life. I thank you for all that you do, that I can see you do and all the things I can't see you do. God, thank you for giving me life to experience and the freedom to express myself. I now know and feel that I am loved by you.

Show Him how much you appreciate Him and how grateful you are for the things He does that you might not even be aware of. As the conversation continues, ask Him for health, happiness, love, forgiveness, truth, direction, help, or whatever you believe your heart is telling you to ask you for. After you do that, what comes next might just be one of the most important steps in a conversation with God.

Now it's time to step back from the conversation and to pause and listen. What I normally do for a few moments, is rest my hand on my heart and tune into my heart and feel the answers, the help, and the truth that I have been seeking for. For your heart is the place where God communicates to you. Tune into your truth by tuning into your heart.

As your conversation comes to an end, it is time to close up and give God love and appreciation for taking this moment to listen to you, hear your words, and feel your heart.

It is in this moment I release my hands from my heart and open them and raise them up to offer Him my heart and my love. Then I close it with an "Amen". But everyone has their own way of connecting with God. This is just the way I do it.

As the next day comes and I pray to God again, I make my prayer slightly different than before. I pray about the same things, but I try to do it in a different way. I do this because, just as with a friend or family member, we don't say exactly the same thing every time we speak with them. God doesn't want that either. He doesn't want it to be meaningless and boring.

God likes deep and meaningful conversations. That is why in the Bible, Jesus warned us not to use vain repetition when we talk with God (Matthew 6:7). When we have the same conversations with those whom we love, they become boring and meaningless. Let me give you a quick example:

Have you ever been in a relationship where the two of you text every day? I know I have. How fast does the conversation get boring and lose its meaning and fire? Texting all the time can affect the type of conversation you are going to have with your partner.

That's why when people in relationships text all the time, they seem to feel less connected to one another and lose their fire when they are together. Texting all the time leaves very little room for human connection and deep personal conversations. The same is true when it comes to your relationship with God.

In order to strengthen your relationship with God so that you don't lose that fire and true connection with Him, the best thing for you to do, is to change up the conversation and how you have that conversation with Him.

Kneeling in prayer is the posture normally assumed by many of God's servants when they set aside time to connect and pray to God. In the Bible there are many examples of this type of praying to God. Daniel 6:10, says, "Now when Daniel learned that the decree had been published, he went home to his upstairs room where the windows opened toward Jerusalem. Three times a day he got down on his knees and prayed, giving thanks to his God just as he had done before." There are also more examples in Acts 9:40, 20:36 21:5.

However, know that it is okay if you don't kneel. Think about it; do you ever stand while you are talking with a friend of yours? Of course, you do! You can stand when you talk with God. Luke 18:10-13 states, "Two men went up to the temple to pray, one a Pharisee and the other a tax collector. The Pharisee stood by himself and prayed: 'God, I thank you that I am not like other people—robbers, evildoers, adulterers —or even like this tax collector. I fast twice a week and give a tenth of all I get.' But the tax collector stood at a distance. He would not even look up to heaven, but beat his breast and said, 'God, have mercy on me, a sinner.'"

Growing up, I let the thought of always having to kneel in order to talk to God, stop me from communicating with him. For I believed that the only proper way to communicate to God was to kneel before him. But what I realized was that I was too lazy to kneel, or wasn't in the place to kneel, and that stopped me from praying.

I felt terrible if I prayed and didn't kneel. Don't let it stop you, like it stopped me. Whenever the need to pray comes up and you seek out God's love and help, arise and know it is okay to pray sitting, lying down, driving or walking.

When you need to pray, posture is not what is important. What is important and what truly interests God, is your attitude and your heart when you take a moment to communicate with Him. That is what's important. But when you do have a moment and time to pray, if you are capable, get down on your knees. For when my knees hit the ground, it is an act of greater commitment and surrender, and I find that my prayers become more meaningful and purposeful.

It becomes so much easier to talk to someone as your relationship with him or her grows. So, in order for you to deepen your relationship with God through prayer, you must get to know God.

In the upcoming chapters you will learn how you can get to know God. Many of us, in the beginning of any new relationship, aren't who we truly are deep down. We are afraid of being judged. We are not sure what we should talk about or what the person across from us might be interested in listening to. We don't want to sound stupid, or too smart, or act too funny. We put on a mask that covers up who we truly are.

The same is true when it comes to your first few conversations with God. You will find that you are not sure what to say. You may feel fearful, judged, or unworthy. But it is not He who judges you, it is you who judges yourself. But have no fear. God knows that you are trying to learn how to have a conversation with Him.

Everything becomes easier in time. The good thing about God, is that even when you are not clear about what it is you are trying to say, He always knows exactly what you are trying to tell Him. He feels your heart and knows it too. He is a very good listener, and he takes in every word, thought, or feeling that you are dealing with.

He hears our hearts and thoughts no matter how unsure or unclear we are when we try to express to Him our needs, wants, and desires. Therefore, know that you are safe to open up and to let go of the fear of not saying the right thing. For all you need to focus on is learning to talk to God the same way you would talk to a deeply loving, protecting, understanding and caring Father, for that is who and what God is.

31

CONNECT TO GOD THROUGH SILENCE

> 66 "Meditation is like giving a hug to ourselves, getting in touch with that awesome reality in us. While meditating, we feel a deep sense of intimacy with God, a love that is inexplicable."

— PARAMAHAMSA YOGANANDA

If prayer is the best way to talk to God, then what is the best way to listen to God? Meditation. It is true, that no matter what your religious background is or what spiritual beliefs you may have, people from all around the world unanimously agree that meditation is the key that will help you to connect deeply with God.

Meditation has done so much for me, and it can and will do the same for you. It has strengthened my relationship with God by purifying and cleansing my mind from my past mistakes that have made me lose connection with God.

It has helped me to accept many of my personal mistakes and has been the number one way in which I have learned to forgive myself and others. By meditating daily, I have noticed that it has effectively removed many of my negative thoughts, strengthened my mind to endure tough times and has enabled me to accept and move in love more freely and abundantly.

It has helped me remove many of my cares, worries, and stresses that have damaged my quality of life, and it has opened the doorway to receive more wisdom and guidance from God. Practicing meditation has helped me to experience an inner transformation that has allowed me to easily hear God when I ask Him for wisdom and knowledge. It has helped me gain access to the key that allows me to open the door to deep spiritual truths.

WHAT IS MEDITATION

Over the past several years, meditation has come into the spotlight. There are so many different articles, podcasts, books and teachers that focus on the benefits of meditation. And yet, throughout my years of teaching other people the power of meditation, there are still all kinds of resistance to the practice.

The most common excuses I have found throughout my years are, "I don't have the time," "I can't quieten my mind," "I can't sit still," and "Meditation is for yogis and spiritual people." Does any of this sound familiar to you? Are you someone who doesn't have the time or who can't seem to sit still?

I know it was rather different at the beginning, but yet this never stopped me from developing a very powerful practice. And I hope it won't stop you either.

To help you build a deeper and loving connection with God, I am here to crush the myth that meditation is difficult and not for you because you are not a "super spiritual person."

Meditation is for everyone and it isn't something that has to take much time, energy or even effort. If you want to learn how to develop a powerful and loving relationship with The Big Three (yourself, others and God) all at the same time, you should learn to meditate!

Meditation is just a practice that is used to train your mind. It is a practice where an individual uses a technique such as mindfulness, or focuses their mind on a particular object, thought or activity to train attention and awareness, and achieve a mentally clear and emotionally calm and stable state of being.

Meditation isn't about becoming a different person, a new person, or even a better person. It's just about training in awareness and getting a healthy sense of perspective. **The stronger your awareness becomes and the healthier your sense of perspective is, the stronger your relationships with yourself, others and God will become.**

Just like finding the way you connect with God, you should find a way you like to meditate. There are so many different ways to meditate and I am sure you use one of those ways right now without even knowing it.

Did you know cooking or listening to music can be and is a form of meditation? How cool is that? Some of the most popular meditation practices in the United States is Transcendental Meditation.

Transcendental Meditation is normally practiced twice a day for twenty minutes a day. During this time, you sit comfortably with your eyes closed and silently repeat a mantra. A mantra is a word or a sound that you repeat throughout your meditation practice that will help you focus the mind.

The word mantra comes from Sanskrit. *Man* is the root of the word for "mind," and *tra* is the root of the word for "instrument." I have found mantras very helpful to relax my mind, find peace and connect deeper to God.

Mantras can help us all disconnect from that stream of never-ending thoughts that are constantly flowing through our minds that could sometimes cause us to feel worried, anxious, stressed, depressed and overwhelmed.

The best way to take control of these negative emotions and states of being and reconnect back with God is to practice meditation. Like I stated before, there are many different ways in which you can meditate, Transcendental Meditation being one of them.

Another popular way people like to practice meditation in the United States is a practice called mindfulness meditation. This type of meditation is based on stillness and calming the mind. Mindfulness meditation often involves sitting comfortably and paying attention to your breath, your physical sensations and your environment. When your mind wonders, you gently bring it back to the present.

What I enjoy doing in this meditation is focus my attention on my heart by placing my hands over my heart and begin to sense the love that is always present. Once I begin to feel this love, I acknowledge that I am connecting and feeling God's presences.

There are so many great benefits of meditation which include: decreased stress and anxiety, increased mental clarity and better sleep. It even helps you feel a true loving connection with God. I've been meditating since 2014 and I owe my joy, my health and my powerful and loving relationships with myself, others and God to this one simple tool!

Through my meditation practices I have learned how to overcome sickness, boost my immune system, forgive myself, others, and God, release my fears, heighten my intuition and open my heart to love again. My daily meditation practice has given me an internal power that supports all that I create and bring forth in the world.

If you want to live a better quality of life and build powerful and loving relationships with The Big Three, you should begin a meditation practice today! I know this is a huge promise. I know it might scare you to believe that through meditation you will feel one with God or be able to love again. I know it might sound intimidating at first. But even if you are someone who has never meditated a day in your life, or if everything you have tried so far has left you feeling frustrated, I want you to know something. Meditation is a practice for everyone! That includes you. You deserve to experience this powerful and deep connection with yourself, others, and God. You can experience this by following the simple meditation steps outlined below.

Remember that we call meditation a "practice" because that is all that it is. It is a habit. You can begin to experience all the amazing benefits and a new connection to yourself, others and God right away. And over time, you will grow even closer to yourself, others, and God.

A SIMPLE MEDITATION

 "Spiritual meditation is the pathway to Divinity. It is a mystic ladder which reaches from earth to heaven, from error to truth, from pain to peace."

— James Allen

Here are a few simple steps that you can follow to connect with God:

1. Find a quiet place. I like to lie in my bed and get comfortable.
2. Close your eyes if you want. I always close my eyes, for it helps me to feel more focused.
3. I always use peaceful music on YouTube. I like to search for the feelings that I am after, which are

peace and love. So, I search for peaceful meditation
music.

4. I put on my headphones and get comfortable in
   my bed.
5. You will notice a mixture of positive and negative
   thoughts running through your mind. At this
   point, you will still be pondering all of your "to-
   do's."
6. Accept it as it is. Just relax and keep calm inside.
   Ask each of your thoughts to go away for a while.
   Believe me, they can listen to you.
7. Now you are ready to have a conversation and
   connect with God.
8. See Him as a point of light in front of you. See Him
   as your father or friend. Picture Him in any way
   you can best connect with.
9. Now talk to Him. Share your truth with Him. Ask
   Him the questions you want answers to.
10. Listen to Him by listening to your heart and you
    will get all the answers. You will find Him
    answering some questions immediately. Some of
    your questions will find answers via another source
    while working throughout the day.
11. Ask Him to give you power to cope with certain
    issues if you are feeling weak.
12. Imagine rays of light coming into you. You will feel
    powerful and strong.
13. Give thanks to God and open your eyes. You can
    feel the Divinity.

THE HEALING POWER

While going through a very tough loss and some difficult
stomach problems that no doctor could seem to figure out, I
decided to do myself a favor and dive into the knowledge
and practice of meditation. As I began this daily practice,

what I found was life changing.

I realized how much it has helped me to slow down my mind's worries, helped me reduce stress, ease my anxiety, and shatter many of my fears. **I started to realize that the deeper I went into my meditation, the more I could hear and be with God.** Then I realized the more I could hear and be with God, the more I felt like I had purpose and my life began to feel so much more meaningful.

As I laid in my bed, deepening my meditation practice and connecting with God, I realized that God was with me, and He could heal my painful stomach issues that I had been suffering through for almost two years. Through meditation, I could heal my broken heart and my physical health.

Meditation has opened up my world and, more importantly, my heart to hear and feel my loving God. Meditation is truly the best way that you can listen and feel God and his inexplicable love.

I promise, that if you ever need wisdom, knowledge, higher guidance, healing, or divine answers, meditation will be your simple solution and you will realize the same thing I realized; through meditation God speaks to your heart and can heal all your struggles.

Meditation is a tool that will improve your physical and mental health. It will help you to increase your focus, eliminate worry, give you a peace of mind and open your heart. Look it up for yourself. What you find will amaze you so much, that it will make you want to take action today!

There are so many endless benefits to meditation, and the greatest benefit is how it helps us to deeply connect and listen to God. This tool will help you eliminate loneliness, emptiness, and suffering.

In our world today, we are more connected with people than ever before. We can FaceTime and Skype anyone we want, yet many of us still feel disconnected, alone, and empty. Why? The reason I believe many of us are still feeling disconnected, alone and empty, is because we are all longing for a true, deep and loving relationship with people instead of with God. People are too unreliable, and they don't always have the love or answers that we are seeking.

Don't get me wrong, I know how important our family, friends and loved ones are to our lives. They make it so much more vibrant and fulfilling. But even when we are with them, we still feel a certain lack of satisfaction.

The ultimate satisfaction and love can be felt when you connect and listen to God through meditation. There have been many times in my life that I would go to other people within my family or within my inner circle and ask them for advice that would make me feel as though I have made the right decision.

However, during the times that I went to others to seek out advice, what I realized was people have many different perspectives, and no one offered advice that felt right for me, or made me feel true to myself. I realized that the advice I got from them was what they would do if they were in my shoes, and that the two of us are different. They haven't been in my shoes and I haven't been in theirs.

So, in order to find the truest answers, I would turn to meditation and seek out wisdom from God. For the truth can be found by asking a few questions, and those question can only be answered by God, not by others. God knows my path, and God knows yours. When dealing with frustration, confusion, stress, and uncertainty, I ask that you seek God and put Him first.

I ask that you build your relationship with him by meditating and listening to Him while you sit in silence. For the Bible states that, "If any of you lacks wisdom, you should ask of God, who gives generously to all without finding fault, and it will be given to you." (James 1:5).

Seek God first through meditation and hear His truth and feel His love. He is there for you and has always been there with you. But you must learn to bring peace to the mind, calm to the body, and rest to the spirit in order to sense his presence. That is when you will find the answers and build the relationship which you have been longing for.

It is true that if you get connected with the Divine power of God, that He will show you the right direction and the correct answer. When you find those answers and build that relationship with God through meditation, you must be willing to trust in God. Trust in him, for he wants what is best for you. When you do, you will notice that your relationship with Him will become clearer and truer in your life.

32

FINDING YOUR WAY

> 66 "True connection with God will begin the moment you move your heart away from self-centeredness and open it up to God-centeredness."
>
> — TYLER JOE STRATTON

I am not an expert on spirituality, and I am not an expert on the Bible. I have been a man who has questioned God, walked away from God, ignored God, used His name in vain, and gone against His Word. I am a sinner. I am not trying to steer you down a path that you are not ready to accept or feel comfortable with. I am just a man who is trying to help you receive the love and relationships you deserve in your life.

My relationship with God has been everything but perfect. But my imperfections are also a part of me, and I honor all of my imperfections and struggles with full responsibility. We all have our own stories, our own paths, and our own ways of connecting and building a relationship with God.

If you are unsure how to connect with God or feel unworthy to have a deep and meaningful relationship with God, know that it is okay to feel that way. We all feel this way at times. Many of us feel too unworthy most of the time and that is what stops us from feeling the love and connection that God is always giving to us. So, for those of you who are struggling to build this relationship and feeling disconnected, I am going to offer you some of the discoveries that I have made that have helped me repair my relationship with God. These discoveries have helped me find a meaningful and everlasting love.

These discoveries have helped me become so much more open to hearing Him and feeling Him in ways I never thought I would experience.

Throughout my journey I have learned a lot. I have learned that church for me isn't always the way I connect to God. But I do enjoy connecting with people who are at whatever church I attend. So, for me, church isn't always the way, but other times it is. If I feel like I need that community in my life, I go to church and if I feel like I don't need a community to strengthen my relationship with God, but I still need God, I sit in silence.

I have learned that sometimes it is when I sit in silence without distraction that I really begin to feel and hear God talk to me. I have learned while sitting in this silence that it's our awareness of God's presence that makes us truly know He is here with us at all times. Which means that when we lose our awareness of God's presence, we lose the connection to God.

Your awareness of God is key to building a deeply connected relationship with God. Another thing I learned along the way was that the awareness of God's presence is not making God become present, it's becoming aware of the presence that already exists. In other words, when it comes to deeply connecting to God, you must learn to raise your awareness of God's presence that already exists and has always existed within.

The only reason you aren't as strongly connected to God as you could be is because of your awareness. Some of us see God as an almighty and powerful God who we can never please. Some of us see a perfect God who we fear because we are so imperfect and have so many faults. Some of us see Him as a father or even a best friend, and some don't even see Him at all. No matter how you see Him, we all can learn how to find our specific way in which we feel seen, connected and loved by God.

Maybe the way you were brought up wasn't the way in which you connect with Him. Don't be afraid to let go of the past and open up to new ways to connect with God. If you aren't able to let go and connect with God your way because you are afraid of what other people or your family might think of you, know this; This is your life. This is your journey and your journey will become so much better for you and for them if you learn the way you connect to God.

We all have different paths in life and don't always travel down the same road as our family and friends do. The same should happen when learning the way in which you connect and build a relationship with God. Knowing that your way could be a different way than those you are around is just as okay as their way.

I ask you to open your mind and heart up and experiment and find your way in which you connect with God. Discovering how you connect to God will really improve the quality of life you live because you will begin to have the faith needed to know that God truly has your back and is working in your favor.

When it came to discovering the different ways in which I connected to God, it was very frustrating, challenging and hopeless at times. I got to the point where I began to believe there was no God. So, don't get too discouraged if it takes some time for you to connect back to God.

Many people visit holy places, read the Bible or other forms of scripture. Some pray to Him, some chant mantras, some offer spiritual rituals and practices that will help them connect with their God. Some find God in nature and others find Him in Church.

Different people believe in different ways of connecting with God, and I am here to say that I believe that there is only one way to truly connect with Him. That way is whatever way you believe is right for you! That is the best way! I believe the only way to connect with God is to understand what feels right for you. I am different from you, and you are different from me, and that is perfectly okay. So how I connect with God and how you connect with God are both acceptable.

The most important and effective way to build a relationship with God is to make sure that whatever method you find useful, you nurture it as much as you can. Because in this day and age, we all need a lot more of God in our everyday lives.

The way I found a more connected relationship with God was when I learned to disconnect from everyone and everything else and learned to quiet my inner world. That is right, I have built a relationship with God and felt His love and His word through stepping away from the outer world and stepping into my inner world.

Meditation is the best way for me to connect with God and hear and feel his love. Have the courage to step away and disconnect to reconnect and you just might feel the true essence of spiritual liberation.

33

FINAL DISCOVERIES

   "In the end all there will ever really be is God in me."

— TYLER JOE STRATTON

For all the men and women out there, who are seeking for a deep and meaningful relationship, hear me out. If a man or a woman isn't following God, they are not fit to lead another. If they do not have a relationship with God, they won't know how to have a true relationship with another. If they do not know who God is, then understand that they do not know what real love is.

Our lives will continue to be based upon the relationship we build with others. God has created in us a need for friends and companionship. He knows that the greatest gift anyone can receive from another is true love and companionship.

To wrap up the final section of this book, I would like to give you a simple, yet very effect way to build and maintain a powerful and loving relationship with God. Here are the five top discoveries I have found that will help you to live your fullest life by creating a powerful and loving relationship with God. Some of these are a recap because they are very important for building your relationship with God.

Discovery #1: To create a powerful and loving relationship with God: You must communicate with God through prayer.

When it comes to building a relationship with God, you must start spending time with Him in prayer. Praying regularly is a powerful way to stay in communication with God and receive regular guidance, support and love.

Throughout the years, I have found it very hard for me to communicate with God, for I am a visual person. I like to know that I have the attention of the person who I am talking to, by means of eye contact. However, when it came time for me to build my relationship with God and learn to talk to Him, I never really felt like I had a connection to Him or that He was listening to me, because I couldn't see Him. It's tough to have a conversation with someone who never seems to talk back or even seems to be there with you.

Not being able to see God kept me from praying to Him because I just never felt as though I was being listened to. For me it was hard to talk to someone who just never seemed to be there. Physically, that is. I never liked when I was trying to talk to someone, and they didn't seem to listen or pay attention to what I had to say. It frustrates me, and it either makes me upset or I begin to lose the energy to keep the conversation going.

That is why when it came to communicating with God, I found it to be difficult because for the longest time, I felt like I was talking to a wall. I was talking, but no one was there to listen. So, I just slowly began to give up on praying and communicating to God for a good while. That is, until I discovered a very powerful teaching that has helped me talk to God daily without feeling like I wasn't being listened to.

You see, growing up in the nineties, before smart phones

came out and new technologies like Skype, Google Hangouts, and Facetime, there was no way of seeing a person when communicating with them on the phone. I remember the only way that I was able to communicate with others was by telephone.

I grew up during a time when talking on the telephone was the only way that I could talk to someone who was long distance. Heck, I even remember the times when I would talk to someone on the telephone for hours or put the telephone on speaker phone as my friends and I would play online computer games together. Sometimes while we were on speaker, minutes would pass without conversation, but we still knew that the other was on the line.

That is when I realized that God is like talking to someone on the telephone. Even though we can't see the other person who is on the other end, we know that they are still there with us.

When communicating on the telephone we talk and they listen, then they talk, and we listen. The same is true when you are in prayer with God. He is on the other end of the telephone when you call out to Him. Don't let the thought of Him not being there stop you from picking up the phone, giving Him a call and starting the conversation.

If you are having a tough time communicating with God because you never feel like He is there, just imagine that you are communicating with Him through a telephone. This helped me a lot. Just because you can't see Him doesn't mean He isn't there and listening to you and feeling your every word.

Discovery #2: To create a powerful and loving relationship with God, you must let Him communicate back to you, and you must listen to Him.

Keep in mind what a conversation is like on the telephone. You talk and they listen; they talk, and you listen. God likes to talk to you a lot more than you are willing to listen to Him. You can hear Him best when you are silent and in a meditative state of being or in complete solitude.

God's most common form of communication is through feeling. Feeling is the language of the soul. If you want to know what's true for you about something or what God is saying to you, look to how you're feeling about it. Feelings can be difficult to discover and often even more difficult to acknowledge.

Yet I have learned that in your total silence, you can find hidden in your deepest feelings your highest truth. I have also come to learn that God also likes to communicate with thought. Thoughts and feelings are not the same, although they can occur at the same time. In communicating with thought, God often use images and pictures. For this reason, thoughts are more effective than mere words as tools of communication. In addition to feelings and thoughts, God also uses the vehicle of experience as a grand form of communication.

And finally, when feelings and thoughts and experiences all fail, God uses words. Words are really the least effective form of communication. To God, they are the most open to misinterpretation, most often misunderstood. God talks to you throughout the entire day, but you need to have an open heart that is ready and willing to feel what He has to say and how He is trying to communicate it to you.

If you really want to hear God a lot more, then you must make it your duty to get to know and recognize His work. You can find His word written in the Bible and many other spiritual texts. Read the Bible like you read every other book. Read it to become informed and enlightened.

This book is packed full of amazing stories that will help you see God's work throughout everyday life. Find time to study the Bible so that God can show you His Work, His love and His relationship He has and wants to have with you.

I have an amazing app on my iPhone called "Bible", and it

has the Bible in an audio version. Take time to listen to the Bible and you will find that your relationship with God will improve dramatically. The more you allow God's word to speak truth, love and hope into your heart, the more you will feel the Divine connection and support God has to offer to each and every one of us.

"Keep this Book of the Law always on your lips; meditate on it day and night, so that you may be careful to do everything written in it. Then you will be prosperous and successful. Have I not commanded you? Be strong and courageous. Do not be afraid; do not be discouraged, for the Lord your God will be with you wherever you go."—*Joshua 1:8-9*

I wanted to add this little passage as a reminder that God will be with you wherever you go so do not think as I have thought and believed that God is not there with you wherever you go. You are loved deeply and supported strongly by God. For God is with you and within you and will always have your back. Trust in God and know that the Universe in which God created has your back.

Discovery #3: To create a powerful and loving relationship with God, we must learn to disconnect, to reconnect.

Meditating will help you deepen your focus as well as help you understand whatever it is you need to learn. There have been so many times in my life where I have heard a good Sunday morning teaching that has lifted my spirit and has enlightened my being while listening to it.

But as the day continues on and the hours slip by, so does the Sunday morning teaching that I just heard, and I can't seem to remember a word that the preacher spoke. How many times have you heard a great sermon and then, a few hours later, can't seem to remember anything about it?

Our world today has programed our minds in a way that makes it harder and harder for us to focus in on one thing and let whatever it is we are focusing on really sink into our minds.

We live in a world today that allows us to see and learn about everything we want but remember nothing. This worries me. For isn't it through the teaching and experiences which we learn and live, that allow us to reach a greater quality of life? Why are so many of us missing the teachings, lessons, and the beautiful and loving connection with God?

There is an endless amount of reasons why so many of us are forgetting everything, from the Sunday morning sermon to what we had to eat yesterday. But the main reason we are not letting the connection with God and the teachings from others sink in, is because we seem too afraid to be alone with our thoughts long enough to let the connection to take place or allow the lesson to sink in.

This world is full of distractions, and what has happened, is we no longer allow our minds to idle or quieten down long enough to ponder what it is we have just learned, or what has just happened. And this causes us to feel uncomfortable or afraid to sit alone in silence with our thoughts. Think about it: What happens as soon as you enter your house? You sit down, check your phone, turn on the tv, and mindlessly watch whatever catches your attention. Many have chosen this routine in everyday life because the truth is, turning on Netflix is so much easier than turning on our minds to ponder a teaching, or sitting down and create that loving connection with God.

That connection with God can be found when you allow yourself to be alone with your thoughts. Your relationship with God will become more powerful and loving once you learn the art of meditation. To meditate, is to deeply think through and ponder something, which, for the most part, is about giving yourself time to let go of all your thoughts and worries and focus on one thing.

This one thing for me is usually one of three things. The first thing I usually like to focus on is my breath, the second thing I like to hold my attention on is my emotions and the third thing I like to focus on is a prayer.

So, find what it is you like to focus on so that you too can silence your thoughts, worries, and mad mind. This one thing for you could be your breathing or finding the tension and stress that you are holding within your body, or even a prayer.

However, in this case, you should focus on The Word of God. For it is full of powerful verses that you should meditate on. It is one thing to set time aside each day to read through the Bible, but it is another to meditate on a passage or verse.

Find time to close your eyes and ponder how great God truly is. This is the time where you can read passages out of the Bible or find a quote online that relates to God, and allow yourself to think about it, question it and understand it deeply.

Think about how loving and kind God is. Count all the blessings God has given you. Thank God for all the gifts He has given you. Meditate on John 3:16; "For God so loved the world, that he gave his only Son, that whoever believes in him should not perish, but have eternal life." Ponder how great God's love is. Feel the love begin to boil in your heart and let love be your pathway to God. Give it a chance. Give it a try.

Allow yourself to be vulnerable and open to possibility. Allow yourself to become more open toward The Word of God and meditate on it day and night if you are serious about building a connection and powerful relationship with Him.

In Joshua 1:8, he talks about how often we are to meditate; "This Book of the Law shall not depart from your mouth, but you shall meditate on it day and night, that you may observe to do according to all that is written in it. For then you will make your way prosperous, and then you will have good success." Meditation will deeply internalize God's way of life within you.

The more you meditate the more you will feel alive and

God's being within you. It will help you build a powerful and loving relationship with God that your heart has been seeking to find. It will help you understand that we are all one and are all created by love, for love, and to never stop giving love.

Go after it, for there will come a time in your life that God may be the only one you will be able to turn to and hold on to. Trial is ahead for all of us. Heartbreak, death, and tragedy will happen, but you don't have to face them alone. God will always be there with you and for you. Build your trust and relationship with God through meditation so you never have to feel so alone again. He is waiting.

Discovery #4: To create a powerful and loving relationship with God, you should allow yourself to experience fasting.

Fasting, by definition, is going without food and/or drink for a period of time. The practice of fasting has so many amazing benefits for the mind, body and spirit. I highly recommend that you try it.

The practice of fasting is mentioned numerous times in the Bible in order for people to draw closer to God. By denying yourself food and water for a time, fasting will remind you of a great truth; You will die without physical sustenance.

Likewise, you will also die spiritually if you do not have spiritual nourishment. Without spiritual food (the living Word of God) you will lose your connection with God.

God wants you to grow with Him and ask for His help. He wants you to fast so that you can learn some amazing spiritual lessons. When you fast, you will become physically weak.

This is a lesson which will teach you that you are only human, and your body is frail. It will remind you that you are mortal, and that without food and water, your body will die. This is a great teaching that I try to learn once per month. Yes, that is right. I try to fast for twenty-four hours without food or water, once per month for multiple reasons.

One of my biggest reasons is to always keep in the back of my mind that I am mortal and my time here is limited. This awareness helps me to understand that each day is a gift and shouldn't be taken for granted.

Your fasting experience will be different than mine, but I do know that you will learn that without God, you will die spiritually. We are all very dependent on God's beautiful creations. From the Earth, to the soil, the rain, and everything we need in order to sustain our physical lives while we are here on this Earth. By allowing yourself to fast, you will build a powerful and loving relationship with God.

You will grow your trust in Him, for He will help you overcome and sustain your spiritual life. Fasting will help you to humble yourself before God and before others. It will help you seek His love, forgiveness, comfort, help, guidance and strength that you will need in order to get through the difficult journeys you will face throughout your life. Fasting is truly one of the greatest tools which God has given to you, so that you may live through Him and be more like Him. It is a tool that will help you to gain a stronger relationship with Him, as well as develop a heart that is humble.

I am not a doctor. So please understand that, while fasting is an excellent tool for spiritual growth, it is not a good thing for everyone to do. Those with diabetes or similar serious health conditions would be wise to seek professional advice before attempting to fast. Please be sure to do your own research and consult your doctor before pursuing this.

To learn more about how to fast, please make sure to check out my podcast on iTunes called, "Ultimate Human Connect Podcast". I will show you more helpful ways to fast, as well as many other ways to build a powerful and loving relationship with yourself, others, and God.

Discovery #5: To create a powerful and loving relationship with God, you must trust in God.

Worrying and stressing never seemed to change anything for me. But trusting in God changed everything for me. I know it is hard to build trust in anyone or anything that has betrayed you and hurt you, but I promise that if you can keep trusting in God, your life will change for the better. Just like mine and millions of others have.

God is always in control, even when your circumstances may seem out of control. God truly does have a reason for allowing things to happen to you or in my eyes, happen for you.

You may never understand why He allows some things to happen, or you may never understand His wisdom, but you must trust in Him, for He knows what is best for you. Let the darkness strengthen you by trusting in God and if you find it hard to trust in the unseen, I hope you can connect to what Nicky Gumbel has written. "Just because you can't see the air, doesn't mean you stop breathing. And just because you can't see God, doesn't mean you stop believing."

Listen, every heart which earnestly asks, which is the path to God? It is shown. Each one of you is given a heartfelt truth. A heartfelt truth isn't something that is seen but something that is felt. Come to Me along the path of your heart, not through a journey of your mind. For you will never find God in your mind, He will only be felt in your heart.

In order to build a powerful and loving relationship with God and to truly know God, you have to get out of your mind and in touch with your heart.

It took me a long time before I was able to do this. I am still working on it and find it to be a daily challenge. However, with consistent effort, a beautiful and peace-filled life has awaited me every time I left my mind and entered in to my heart.

When I take my focus off my mind and put my awareness

on my heart, life seems to be working for me rather than against me. When I follow my heart and stay in touch with it, I believe God becomes so much easier to trust. Walking with God in my heart has helped me to feel supported, loved, and guided.

Trust in God and you will find your life and your relationships with others become so much more peaceful, enjoyable and loving. For when you trust in God with an open heart, the right people, the right job and the right life are bestowed upon you. You will begin to enjoy the full life that is waiting for you.

Trust in God when you are going through the darkness and the struggle. Find the light by finding your heart. I know that there are just some things in which you can't take on by yourself, and that is when you should allow God to help you so that you can get through whatever it is you are going through. But first you must tune into your heart and feel His existence.

Therefore, I ask that you don't take on those mountainous struggles and darkened times alone. Let go and trust in your heart to guide you back to God. For when you truly let go and tune into your heart, trusting in God will become second nature. Even while life seems to be pushing you off the edge of difficulty and struggle, there are only two things that will come out of it when you allow yourself to fall into your heart and trust in God; He will either catch you when you fall, or He will teach you how to spread your wings and soar.

Relationships have always been built from your heart and on trust, and the same goes for the relationship you have with God. You must put your heart to the test and your trust in Him, for He is there to help you even when things might seem hard and tragic.

He is there with you, so open your heart and put your trust, faith and belief in Him. Everything is possible when you allow God in your heart. Live from your heart not your mind. Live from your heart not your hurt.

By putting God ahead of everyone and everything else in your life, all other things will fall into their proper places. Your life will begin to change when you put Him first. Success will come. Love will be chiseled into your heart and your life will open up for you and become a life worth remembering. Let go and trust in God, for He is the way to building a deeper love for yourself, powerful relationships with others and living your life to the fullest.

 "Love to me is Godly, and God to me is Love. That is why Love is Everything."

— Tyler Joe Stratton

FINAL WORDS

If you found this book helpful, encouraging, supportive or uplifting, please make it your mission to tell others about it. I believe it is on each one of us to spread positivity and empowerment during these times of chaos, negativity and turmoil.

You have the power to be the dealer of hope by lifting up other people through positive education so that their life begins to change for the better.

If there is one thing that I'd ask any of you to do, it would be to be the light in the darkness, be the hope in the hopeless, and be the love that you know this world needs.

Remember, it is our duty and grand plan to be the warrior whose mission it is to love, lead, and serve all those that we can, by being the person they need you to be. And you can be that person in their life simply by sharing this book with those you know who need some help, hope, love, and encouragement.

And with all the love in the world and with the upmost gratitude in my heart, I thank you for spending your precious time with me and reading this book! Be sure to head over to Instagram and give me a follow @tylerjoestratton so that we can connect and talk about the book and the ways in which we can come together and help one another impact more lives!

LOVE. LEAD. SERVE.

Tyler Joe Stratton

RESOURCES

INSTAGRAM: @tylerjoestratton
FACEBOOK: Tyler Joe Stratton
YOUTUBE: Tyler Joe Stratton
WEBSITE: https://linktr.ee/tylerjoestratton
PODCAST: The Ultimate Human Connect Podcast

REFERENCES

A quote by Alexander Pope. (n.d.). Retrieved June 20, 2020, from https://www.goodreads.com/quotes/36806-blessed-is-he-who-expects-nothing-for-he-shall-never

A quote by Harvey MacKay. (n.d.). Retrieved June 20, 2020, from https://www.goodreads.com/quotes/79511-time-is-free-but-it-s-priceless-you-can-t-own-it

A quote by Ken Keyes Jr. (n.d.). Retrieved from https://www.goodreads.com/quotes/331046-a-loving-person-lives-in-a-loving-world-a-hostile

A quote by Remington Miller. (n.d.). Retrieved June 14, 2020, from https://www.goodreads.com/quotes/7969069-i-found-i-was-more-confident-when-i-stopped-trying

A quote by Rudy Francisco. (n.d.). Retrieved June 14, 2020, from https://www.goodreads.com/quotes/8302061-perhaps-we-should-love-ourselves-so-fiercely-that-when-others

Agyei, S. (2018, June 8). Theodore Roosevelt. Retrieved June 20, 2020, from https://medium.com/@steveagyeibeyondlifestyle/the-most-important-single-ingredient-in-the-formula-of-success-is-knowing-how-to-get-along-with-4f3babdc6c55

Ashe, T. (n.d.). Nelson Mandela. Retrieved June 14, 2020, from https://blogs.shu.edu/diplomacyresearch/2013/12/11/an-exemplar-of-forgiving-prisoner-nelson-mandela/

Ate, T. (2019, July 16). How Jim Carrey Made $20m By Using The Law of Attraction. Retrieved June 14, 2020, from https://addictedtoeverything.com/success/how-jim-carrey-made-20m-by-using-the-law-of-attraction/

Bob Proctor Quote: "You are God's highest form of creation. You are a living breathing creative magnet. You have the ability to control what..." (n.d.). Retrieved June 14, 2020, from https://quotefancy.com/quote/1707996/Bob-Proctor-You-are-God-s-highest-form-of-creation-You-are-a-living-breathing-creative

Burchard, B. (2014, December 21). Be Great in Relationships. Retrieved June 20, 2020, from https://brendonburchard.tumblr.com/post/105785812578/be-great-in-relationships

Burchard, B. (2017, March 25). Brendon Burchard - Live. Love. Matter. Retrieved from https://www.facebook.com/brendonburchardfan/photos/a.417731891593777/1468162816550674/?type=3&theater

Burchard, Brendon. (2014, March 15). Dealing with Fate; Deciding on Destiny. Retrieved June 14, 2020, from https://brendonburchard.tumblr.com/post/79663552596/dealing-with-fate-deciding-on-destiny

Chopra, D. (n.d.). Ask Deepak: Understanding the Power of Desire. Retrieved June 14, 2020, from http://www.oprah.com/spirit/understanding-the-power-of-desire-ask-deepak

Chopra, D. (2005). *Synchrodestiny : Harnessing the Infinite Power of Coincidence to Create Miracles* (New Ed). London, United Kingdom: Ebury Pr.

Chopra, Deepak . (2019, November 7). 5 Steps to Setting Powerful Intentions. Retrieved June 14, 2020, from https://chopra.com/articles/5-steps-to-setting-powerful-intentions

Communication Is The Fuel That Keeps The Fire Of Your Relationship Burning, Without It, Your Relationship Goes Cold. – William Paisley. (n.d.). Retrieved June 21, 2020, from http://quotespictures.com/communication-is-the-fuel-that-keeps-the-fire-of-your-relationship-burning-without-it-your-relationship-goes-cold-william-paisley/

D, J. (2017, February 11). Tony Robbins on How To Master Relationships. Retrieved June 20, 2020, from http://sourcesofinsight.com/how-to-master-relationships/

Daniels, E. (2019, November 14). Jim Carrey's 5 Tips for Creating Your Reality. Retrieved June 14, 2020, from https://www.applythelawofattraction.com/jim-carrey-law-attraction/

Eckhart Tolle. (2010, January 24). Jim Carrey On The Power Of Intention [Video file]. In *YouTube*. Retrieved from https://www.youtube.com/watch?v=8qSTHPABoHc

Feinberg, M. (2019, October 16). 5 Ways to Jumpstart Your Prayer Life This Week. Retrieved June 21, 2020, from https://churchleaders.com/smallgroups/small-group-articles/175421-5-ways-to-jumpstart-your-prayer-life-this-week.html

Fowler, D. (n.d.). Marriage: A Powerful Heart Drug in Short Supply. Retrieved June 20, 2020, from https://www.asanet.org/sites/default/files/savvy/press/JHSB_March_2012_Idler_News_Release.pdf

Genesis 1 | KJV Bible | YouVersion. (n.d.). Retrieved June 21, 2020, from https://www.bible.com/bible/1/GEN.1.KJV

Gray, J. (1995). *Men are from Mars, women are from Venus* (1St Edition). London, England: HarperCollins .

Green Ingersoll, R. (2019). *Lectures of Col. R.G. Ingersoll - Latest*. Glasgow, Scotland: Good Press.

Henry Ford Quote: "You are the Master of your Fate, the Captain of your Soul." (n.d.). Retrieved from https://quotefancy.com/quote/826076/Henry-Ford-You-are-the-Master-of-your-Fate-the-Captain-of-your-Soul

Hill, N. (2017). *The Law of Success from the 1925 Manuscript Lessons*. U.S.A, U.S.A: BNPUBLISHING.

Hope, J. (2009, July 3). How being married can cut your risk of Alzheimer's in later life. Retrieved from https://www.dailymail.co.uk/health/article-1197191/How-married-cut-risk-Alzheimers-later-life.html

Huffpost. (n.d.). Marriage And Health: Study Suggests Marriage Can Help With Recovery After Heart Surgery. Retrieved from https://www.huffpost.com/entry/marriage-and-health_n_1324509

[Illustration]. (n.d.). *The Power of a Vision*. Retrieved from https://www.pinterest.co.uk/pin/30188259987046062/

Inspiring Quotes. (n.d.). Top 30 quotes of BARRY LONG famous quotes and sayings | inspringquotes.us. Retrieved June 14, 2020, from https://www.inspiringquotes.us/author/2567-barry-long

itsMoti. (2019, August 19). Jim Carrey - Love or Fear - Ask the Universe. [Video file]. In *YouTube*. Retrieved from https://www.youtube.com/watch?v=RP3pFWaw4Kc

James Allen Quote. (n.d.). Retrieved from https://quotefancy.com/quote/1065924/James-Allen-Spiritual-meditation-is-the-pathway-to-Divinity-It-is-a-mystic-ladder-which

James, W. (n.d.). A quote by William James. Retrieved June 20, 2020, from https://www.goodreads.com/quotes/23215-the-deepest-principle-in-human-nature-is-the-craving-to

Maharishi International University. (2014, May 30). Highlights: Jim Carrey's Commencement Address at the 2014 MUM Graduation [Video file]. In *YouTube*. Retrieved from https://www.youtube.com/watch?time_continue=334&v=TV-tA8njqq8&feature=emb_logo

McDowell, E. (n.d.). Emily McDowell Quotes. Retrieved June 14, 2020, from https://www.quotes.net/quote/72457

Merriam-Webster. (n.d.). Forgive. Retrieved June 14, 2020, from https://www.merriam-webster.com/dictionary/forgive

Michael, P. (2020, June 3). Success Secrets: 7 EPIC Law Of Attraction Quotes From Conor McGregor. Retrieved June 14, 2020, from https://medium.com/@philip_michael/success-secrets-7-epic-law-of-attraction-quotes-from-conor-mcgregor-4c07c858db43

Moncur, L. (n.d.). The Quotations Page: Quote from Jim Carrey. Retrieved June 14, 2020, from http://www.quotationspage.com/quote/38175.html

Paramahansa Yogananda Quote. (n.d.). Retrieved June 21, 2020, from https://quotefancy.com/quote/884668/Paramahansa-Yogananda-Meditation-is-like-giving-a-hug-to-our-ourselves-getting-in-touch

Paul, J. (n.d.). A quote by Pope John Paul II. Retrieved June 21, 2020, from https://www.goodreads.com/quotes/172155-the-worst-prison-would-be-a-closed-heart

Prichard, S. (2017, July 10). 31 Forgiveness Quotes to Inspire Us to Let It Go. Retrieved June 14, 2020, from https://www.skipprichard.com/31-forgiveness-quotes-to-inspire-us-to-let-it-go/

Rexford, S. (2018, May 24). Casey Neistat | Action and Intent — Sarah Rexford. Retrieved June 14, 2020, from https://www.itssarahrexford.com/blog//casey-neistat-action-and-intent

Schwab, J (2019, March 24). Brian Tracy Quotes To Motivate... Retrieved June 20, 2020, from https://www.inspiringalley.com/quotes-by-brian-tracy/

Time is the currency of relationships. If you want to invest into your relationships, start by investing your time. (n.d.). Retrieved June 20, 2020, from https://twitter.com/johnhall/status/1159229736352145408

Tony Robbins Quote: "Remember: we all get what we tolerate. So stop tolerating excuses within yourself, limiting beliefs of the past, or half..." (n.d.). Retrieved June 14, 2020, from https://quotefancy.com/quote/923102/Tony-Robbins-Remember-we-all-get-what-we-tolerate-So-stop-tolerating-excuses-within

Walsch, N. D. (1995). *Conversations With God* (1st ed.). London, Great Britain: Hodder & Stoughton.

Warren, R. (2013). *The Purpose Driven Life: What on Earth Am I Here For?* (3rd ed.). Michigan, America: Zondervan.

William Arthur Ward Quotes. (n.d.). Retrieved June 12, 2020, from https://www.goodreads.com/quotes/60933-if-you-can-imagine-it-you-can-achieve-it-if

Williamson, J. (2017, November 17). 25 Brendon Burchard Quotes to Help You *Bring* the Joy. Retrieved June 14, 2020, from https://healingbrave.com/blogs/all/brendon-burchard-quotes-bring-the-joy

Made in the USA
Middletown, DE
26 September 2020